The POWER of FOUR

ALSO BY JOSEPH M. MARSHALL III

Keep Going

*Soldiers Falling into Camp: The Battles at the Rosebud
and the Little Big Horn* (co-author)

Winter of the Holy Iron

On Behalf of the Wolf and the First Peoples

The Dance House: Stories from Redbud

The Lakota Way: Stories and Lessons for Living

The Journey of Crazy Horse: A Lakota History

How Not to Catch Fish: And Other Adventures of Iktomi

Walking with Grandfather: The Wisdom of Lakota Elders

The POWER of FOUR

LEADERSHIP LESSONS OF
CRAZY HORSE

Joseph M. Marshall III

STERLING

New York / London
www.sterlingpublishing.com

STERLING and the distinctive Sterling logo are registered trademarks of
Sterling Publishing Co., Inc.

Library of Congress Cataloging-in-Publication Data Available

10 9 8 7 6 5 4 3 2

Published by Sterling Publishing Co., Inc.
387 Park Avenue South, New York, NY 10016
© 2009 by Joseph M. Marshall III
Distributed in Canada by Sterling Publishing
c/o Canadian Manda Group, 165 Dufferin Street
Toronto, Ontario, Canada M6K 3H6
Distributed in the United Kingdom by GMC Distribution Services
Castle Place, 166 High Street, Lewes, East Sussex, England BN7 1XU
Distributed in Australia by Capricorn Link (Australia) Pty. Ltd.
P.O. Box 704, Windsor, NSW 2756, Australia

Manufactured in the United States of America
All rights reserved

Sterling ISBN 978-1-4027-4881-3

For information about custom editions, special sales, premium and
corporate purchases, please contact Sterling Special Sales
Department at 800-805-5489 or specialsales@sterlingpublishing.com.

The *The* **POWER** *of* **FOUR**

LEADERSHIP LESSONS OF
CRAZY HORSE

╫

CONTENTS

INTRODUCTION: WHAT IS A LEADER?

D oes having a position of authority automatically make someone a leader? The generally accepted answer to this question seems to be *yes*. What about passionate or persistent espousal of a cause—does that make someone a leader? *Sure*, we say, often buying into someone's "authority" based on the volume of their rhetoric. Yet, according to most dictionaries, the true definition of a leader is "one who leads by influence."

Perhaps most of us are too busy just trying to survive and make a living to focus much attention on how our society functions. To be sure, people in authority will and do have an impact on our everyday lives. The actions and decisions of mayors, board chairmen, governors, chief executives, city council members, state legislators, and members of

Congress affect most if not all of us in one way or another. These people may think of themselves as leaders because of the titles they hold or the authority vested in them, while we ordinary citizens accept them as leaders for no other reason than the jobs they have.

Too often we give people our trust without really knowing what does, or does not, qualify them for the positions they hold. We forget that anyone who runs for public office at any level is, first, a *politician*. Politicians may learn how to get themselves elected, but can they learn how to lead? Similarly, we forget that most people who occupy high-level corporate positions are there to serve the bottom line, for themselves and for the company. Witness the benefits reportedly given to corporate CEOs and the like, who seem to be more lucratively rewarded for not doing their jobs than they are for doing them. Corporate executives know how to make money, or be rewarded for failing do so, but they are not necessarily leaders.

So that demands the question: Can mayors, CEOs, senators, board chairmen, and the like be leaders? Of course they can, but they must rise above themselves and the positions they hold. The fact of the matter, however, is that many of them do not rise above, because people in authority tend to spend much time and effort working to keep their jobs. And they often fail to realize that there is a difference between the appearance and the reality of being a leader.

The word *leader* is often applied too freely. When we confer that label offhandedly, we forget that leadership cannot be mandated by a job description. True leadership is only possible when character is more important than authority—especially the authority to compel or control the actions of others. It is character, and not position, that can turn administrators, directors, supervisors, and even senators, congressmen, governors, and presidents into leaders.

In every society or culture throughout history, people from every walk of life and in every endeavor—good or bad, legal or illegal, moral or immoral, harmful or helpful—have undoubtedly influenced others to do something they may not have done on their own. Does this mean that we should consider Genghis Khan, Adolf Hitler, Mao Tse-tung, Attila the Hun, Ho Chi Minh, or Benito Mussolini to be effective leaders? After all, those men did convince people of the righteousness or necessity of their causes and influence them to follow. It is said that Adolf Hitler led the German people—meaning that they followed willingly on the path of fascism that caused so much death and destruction. Genghis Khan was intent on conquering the world, and nearly did, killing hundreds of thousands of people in the process.

Mao Tse-tung, we are told, led millions and millions of his countrymen through a "cultural revolution" that brought China into the modern world. But we are only now learning of the unspeakable atrocities he caused to be committed against his own people, not so much in the name of change but to maintain his own authority.

Defined broadly, it seems that leaders can be villains as well as heroes, considering the fact that both are able to influence, manipulate, or coerce enough people to follow them that the consequences of their leadership extend far beyond themselves. We must not overlook the fact that any instrument, process, idea, or method that is used to accomplish good can also be used for dark or destructive purposes. Of course, it is also important to remember that a willing follower has just as much of a choice as a leader, and therefore bears the same responsibility. We can only imagine what would have happened, or not happened, had Hitler's words fallen on deaf ears. The lesson here is that in order for societies, cultures, and nations to function and thrive, we must all aid and abet leadership on the side of morality, fairness, equality, and justice. To that end we must demand not so much that our leaders be more than we are as ordinary people, but that they epitomize and apply the best that we are as individuals, nations, societies, and cultures. We have the right to good, ethical, moral, dynamic, and even inspirational leadership. More importantly, we need it.

Back in the mists of time, humans learned the value of working together and the strength in numbers. Organization increased the odds of survival because a group could hunt and gather more efficiently, and protect itself more effectively against danger. At some point, someone took charge, either by the power of persuasion, which required reason, or the force of will, enforced by size and strength. However it occurred, the concept and practice of leadership became part of human existence. Since then, whether by force, assassination, trickery, election, consensus, appointment, or birth right, leaders have ascended to truly serve, to control, or to take advantage. And since that time, humans have wrestled with the issue of what makes a good leader.

Perhaps at this point in our social and cultural development we have refined the ways in which we select people to be in charge; but in terms of people's motivations for wanting to become leaders, not much has changed. The truth is that people sometimes (or too often) seek to lead out of the desire for personal satisfaction or gain. Fortunately, many men and women who occupy positions of leadership and authority have no ulterior motives, and they do or try to do their jobs well. Kind or cruel, able or ineffectual, selfish or selfless, leaders come and go. Some achieve a solid record of accomplishment and serve the greater good, and some accomplish little or serve only themselves. When we consider the recurring themes of human history it becomes clear that none of this is likely to change anytime soon.

This does not mean, however, that we are doomed to suffer or thrive at the whim of those who lead us. Rather, it means that we must begin to take responsibility for our own roles in wielding and yielding to authority.

Back in the pre-reservation days, the Lakota people of the northern plains had the best deterrent to bad leaders: They simply stopped following them. As long as a leader was effective, people followed. If he abused the faith and trust placed in him, the people could turn away from him and there was nothing to be done. We may turn our backs on an ineffectual leader today, but there are the issues such as terms of office to contend with. In the field of health care, preventative measures are considered viable approaches to improve health and well-being; perhaps, in much the same way, more effective methods are in order for assessing our potential leaders. Even without a consistent, organized effort to this effect, it would behoove us ordinary people—who greatly outnumber our elected officials—to develop solid standards to which we hold the people we appoint, select, and elect. Those standards should go beyond academic credentials, political pedigree, party affiliation, or even religious affiliation, and be based strongly on character, first and foremost.

At the very least, a leader should be characterized by the following traits:

Selflessness

A selfless person puts the needs and concerns of others first by making an effort to meet or mitigate them. Perhaps the best example of selflessness was Mother Teresa, who made it her life's work to literally comfort the afflicted. Yet, she also demonstrated another kind of selflessness: She had no personal need for recognition. Obviously the world took notice of her and of her work, but she wisely turned that attention into opportunity for her cause by focusing it toward the need and away from herself. As human beings we have a need for attention and recognition, and we feel good about ourselves when we are singled out and recognized for a job well done. But if we can commit ourselves to a calling without an unreasonable need for recognition, then we can be truly selfless.

Morality

Most of us are able to discern between right and wrong, but sadly this does not necessarily mean that we always choose right. Rather, our ethics are often clouded by circumstances—or at least by our perception of those circumstances.

We should expect our leaders to understand that our societies and cultures must be founded upon and grounded in morality. Furthermore, we should be wary of aspiring leaders who conveniently discover the necessity for morality only at the moment they decide to apply for a job or stand for election. Leaders need to demonstrate their morality in consistent action, not just rhetoric.

Experience

In our image-conscious, youth-oriented society, young and inexperienced men and women are too often given positions of significant responsibility. In many cases organizations make such leadership decisions based on finances alone, as a more qualified senior employee will have achieved a salary level many times higher than a young person can demand. On the other hand, young and inexperienced people are easier to influence and even control. Whatever the reason, in these instances valuable experience is cast aside and the organization suffers in the long run, its glitzy, youthful image unable to compensate for the deeper lack of leadership experience.

In pre-reservation days, the Lakota culture had a method that allowed young would-be warriors to gain firsthand experience. By accompanying military excursions and patrols not as full-fledged combatants, but as helpers and observers, they served an apprenticeship that afforded them the opportunity to learn from experienced warriors in the field.

The only antidote to inexperience is time and the accumulation of experience. American society and Western cultures in general have chosen to dispense with experience by ignoring older people. After a certain age these people are considered obsolete at best or, at worst, a burden. Rather than being valued for the wisdom of their acquired life experience, they are retired and put out to pasture. This may be the single most self-defeating mind-set in any society or culture.

Honesty
One has only to tune in to any popular network or cable news program to see yet another politician denying his involvement with the latest political scandal—often in the face of information or evidence to the contrary. Even once they are found guilty, these "leaders" often still assert their innocence. Politicians have certainly taught us that honesty is not synonymous with politics. So, while they may indeed be in positions of great

authority, this lack of commitment to honesty disquali-
fies them from being good leaders.

Yet if the political climate is such that we are not
surprised by the dishonesty of our elected officials, then
perhaps this sad state of affairs is really a reflection on
us. We, the ordinary people who make up the electorate,
have allowed this to happen. And while it is usually too
late to save a politician from himself, we can and must
make an effort to save ourselves by assuring that the
next candidate understands where we stand on the issue
of character. If honesty is one of the basic virtues that
anyone and everyone should live up to, that includes
politicians and elected officials as well as those responsible for putting them into power.

Responsibility

In the course of daily life all of us are responsible for
many things—from getting up and out of bed to face
the day, to performing tasks related to keeping
ourselves and our families functioning and happy, and
doing our jobs to the best of our ability. Most of us as
individuals and as members of our society understand
what being responsible means in terms of demands on
our time, effort, and financial resources, but what we
sometimes overlook is that responsibility also draws on
our values.

We know all too well how long it takes to drive children to school, or how many hours we have to work at our job to afford groceries or the car payment. But all too often we are also confronted with the choice between right and wrong. As we face those choices, the critical part of decision making is not so much a matter of cost in dollars and cents. It is a matter of applying the foundational values we learned from our families and our communities to make a choice that is good and healthy.

Because we are human, we do make mistakes; and when we do, we face another kind of responsibility. Sometimes we must pay for our errors in dollars or time or emotional hardship, but before we do that we must be willing to say, "I made a mistake." Whether living up to that kind of responsibility is any harder, or easier, than working every day or paying bills or caring for our families is not the most important issue. The most important issue is to take responsibility for something that cannot be changed, even after we own up to our error. This is one of the most difficult responsibilities we face as individuals, societies, and nations, but it is also the most necessary. It is incumbent on any leader to take this responsibility seriously and act on it with integrity and commitment.

Power has always been the key to leadership. When it is gained through deception, coercion, threat, or brute force, such power tends to benefit only those who hold it—often to the detriment of their willing or unwilling dependents. Yet, if power can serve the leader, it can also serve the follower.

Many general elections in the United States, for example, feature close races, especially for congressional seats. Sometimes they are decided by less than a few thousand votes. Such narrow margins of victory are a message to the winners, especially incumbents. If, for example, one hundred thousand people vote for the winner but ninety-eight thousand voted for the other candidate or viewpoint, then it is in the elected official's best interest to pay attention to the needs and desires of his or her entire constituency, not just those of supporters. Whoever wins must represent or work for *all* the people, including those who voted for the other candidate. If they do not, then it may well cost them the very power and authority with which they have been entrusted. Yet, if we, like the pre-reservation Lakota people, were to simply refuse to follow bad leaders, then it is unlikely that much positive change would be effected. In fact, the chances are that bad leaders would just continue to act unchecked in their own self-interest. And to merely settle for the "best of all evils" is to give away our power entirely.

Instead, we must reassess our priorities in terms of what we expect from our leaders by redefining our idea of leadership altogether.

This is much easier said than done, of course, because our accepted definitions of leadership have historically been shaped by those who were elected or appointed, or who inherited, assumed, or took control. Part of redefining leadership, then, is to divest ourselves of the notion that the only leaders are people in positions of authority, especially in public service. If we accept the definition that a leader is one who *influences* others, then we should realize that anyone can be a leader. If we accept that premise, then parents, grandparents, teachers, pastors, and rabbis are also understood to be—and empowered as—leaders. As a matter of fact, anyone of character and principle can be a leader when the moment or the situation is right. That would mean, for instance, that the proportionately small number of women currently elected to the U.S. Senate are leaders not only because they are senators, but also because they are part of a growing number of women who seek public service. That is clearly an influence on other women, young and old.

It is better to influence leaders than to empower them. One way to do this is to hold them to realistic standards and expectations. Leaders should fit the requirements set by the group or community that they serve. To set those standards and establish basic requirements, we need to learn a good deal about the factors that make a good leader. One of the best ways to do this is to look to the past and take lessons from the leaders who have served before our time.

Throughout history there have been the despots and demagogues as well as fair-minded and just leaders, and those in between. Societies, cultures, and nations have risen on the backs of good and powerful leaders, and they have fallen because of their leaders' misjudgments, mistakes, and vices. All of these are lessons we should heed. Yet it is often more productive to learn from the positive than to dwell on the negative or reinforce our belief in our own powerlessness.

There have been many good leaders throughout history who, despite their human imperfections, had a depth of experience and strength of character that helped them to succeed. One of those was the Oglala Lakota leader Crazy Horse, who achieved prominence and fame in the latter part of the nineteenth century. This common man was invested with power because his people saw that the characteristics that made him a good man and an exemplary warrior would also make him a good leader.

Crazy Horse did not aspire to leadership, but neither did he turn away from it when he was asked to make a choice. Beyond the good he did for his people during his own time, or even the place he still holds in history, the true legacy of Crazy Horse is the example he set and the lessons he offered to those of us who hold a vision for leadership that uses power in the interest of justice and service.

A Cultural Insight

The number four is extremely important in Lakota culture, for the simple reason that *four* is all around us: west, north, east, and south are collectively referred to as the four corners of the Earth, or the four winds. There are the four seasons—winter, spring, summer, and autumn—and also the four basic elements of life, which are earth, wind, fire, and water. We humans experience four stages of life, namely, infancy, childhood, adulthood, and elder years. And we should not forget the four greatest virtues, generosity, fortitude, bravery, and wisdom.

"Four" is at the very least significant as a concept and organizing principle. But traditional Lakota people believe that it has power. For that reason, we acknowledge and use it in our daily lives. It has been very natural for me, as a Lakota writer, to look at the life of Crazy Horse the man, delve into his persona as a leader, and see the four philosophies he used to be an effective and dynamic leader.

Non-Lakota people have long been fascinated with Crazy Horse, but that interest is primarily related to his exploits and accomplishments as a warrior. That, sadly, is where the perception of him usually begins and ends. As a matter of fact, while men such as Sitting Bull, Gall, Spotted Tail, and Red Cloud are often romanticized as warriors and "chiefs," such perceptions are narrow and one-dimensional, preventing any insight into these great men as more rounded, complex human beings.

All Lakota males fulfilled two necessary societal roles as hunters *and* warriors. To put it another way, they were both providers and protectors. The persona of warrior, then, is only part of the male identity. Both roles were essential for the survival of the entire community, but in different ways.

The stereotype of Indian males as universally "warlike" was probably a consequence of the initial interaction between white and native people. From the very beginning of native and European contact, it was the warrior who white people encountered first and most frequently. This is because when strangers approached, the men took on their duty as warriors to protect and defend, placing themselves between possible danger and their homes and families. What most of the white people didn't see, however—or what lent less drama to their stories—was that when those warriors stepped off the warpath and went home, they were grandfathers, fathers, uncles, heads of households, teachers, storytellers, bow and arrow craftsmen, horse trainers, and so on. Some of them were civilian and military leaders as well. One of those was Crazy Horse.

Non-natives have singled this man out for scrutiny because he was perceived to be responsible for the defeat of Lieut. Col. George Custer in June of 1876. But while Custer did indeed lose his last battle at the Little Bighorn, there were other Lakota and Northern Cheyenne military leaders on the field that day. To clearly understand Crazy Horse's place in history it is necessary to look at his role not only as a warrior, but also as an inspirational and effective leader. To do otherwise is to simply reinforce the stereotype and deny ourselves valuable lessons that are just as viable today as they were during Crazy Horse's time.

Crazy Horse did not teach leadership; he simply demonstrated it. He was influenced by many leaders who had gone before him, as well as by the values espoused by his culture and family. As time went on, he was chosen to be headman over the villages that made up his community because he was a good man and a strong, persistent, compassionate leader. It is for these reasons that the Lakota people will never forget him, and that his legacy has so much to offer those outside the Lakota lineage.

Whatever else Crazy Horse was perceived to be, he was a deeply spiritual man, owing largely to his father's calling as a medicine man and spiritual leader. But he was not spiritual simply because he was led to it. Like most Lakota of the day, he was deeply connected to the environment around him and actively practiced his beliefs—that is, he spent time alone, praying and meditating. He was certainly aware of the significance and the power of four.

Four factors stand out when looking at Crazy Horse the leader—and therein lies a powerful connection between the past and present. These factors or philosophies were the basis for his leadership success:

Know yourself.
Know your friends.
Know the enemy.
Lead the way.

These maxims can be applied today by leaders and nonleaders alike.

Most of us will not be warriors, much less a glorious one like Crazy Horse was; but many of us can be leaders. Of course, there is no magic formula that ensures success. The less we, as leaders *and* followers, complicate the standards and processes by which leaders are developed, chosen, and expected to function, however, the more their success is possible. Most importantly, we must understand that a successful leader is one who works for the good of the many, not just for his or her own interests. By remaining true to his four basic philosophies, Crazy Horse became a great leader in his own time and a model of great leadership for future generations.

There is eloquence in simplicity, and strength as well.

LAKOTA LEADERSHIP

Under a hot June sun in 1876, in the haze of a hanging dust cloud, amidst the hum and ricochet of bullets, the crack of gunfire, the rumble of horses' hooves, and the cries of fighting and dying men, a Lakota warrior was about to prove himself once again on the battleground.

Tasunke Witko, better known to history as Crazy Horse, urged his horse into a flying gallop across the broken ground on the side of what would come to be known as Battle Ridge, and into enemy gunfire. Up until that moment, Gall, a Hunkpapa Lakota and protégé of Sitting Bull, had been largely responsible for the resistance against Custer's five companies. After the American army had fired its initial rounds into the great village, killing two wives and one of his daughters among many others, Gall slashed his shirt in mourning and skillfully orchestrated a running battle. Using the Lakota and Cheyenne fighters' greatest strength—their considerable skills as light cavalry—he led his men to flank the retreating soldiers on both sides and dismantle the attacking units.

Crazy Horse had ridden north through the two-mile-long village after breaking off from the first engagement of the battle, the attack on the southern end of the great encampment now known as the Valley Fight. At his own lodge he took a second horse from his wife and then called for a carefully selected group of warriors to follow. He led this detachment north across the Little Bighorn River, then east to a point north of Battle Ridge. There he positioned his detachment to effectively block the remnants of Custer's forces from pushing beyond the end of the ridge, now infamously known as Last Stand Hill.

As he got a full view of the tactical situation, Crazy Horse saw that one company was holding its own as a cohesive unit at least a couple hundred yards from the end of Battle Ridge. He guided his mount like the point of a deadly arrow toward the knot of stubbornly fighting soldiers, charging against Company I of the U.S. 7th Cavalry. Behind him a hundred warriors watched in sheer amazement, then followed his lead.

They rode with fierce determination, spurred onward by duty, grief for their dead and wounded, and the inspirational force of Crazy Horse's fearless example. Within minutes, the last of Custer's soldiers were eliminated and the second engagement of the Battle of the Little Bighorn was over. Later, one Northern Cheyenne warrior described the final mounted charge when Crazy Horse had ridden well ahead of the rest of his men, totally exposed to enemy gunfire. It was, he said, the bravest thing he had ever seen.

But Crazy Horse was not the only person to act with conspicuous courage that day. Every man in the three engagements of the battle fought with bravery. Back at the encampment of eight to ten thousand people, the mothers and grandmothers courageously gathered the children in the midst of fear and confusion and fled to the north, away from the initial attack. Even many of the older men, fighters well past their physical prime, joined the fight, while those who did not remained behind to serve as the last line of defense for the women and children. Courage was a common virtue that day and into the next.

Yet courage alone would not have won the Battle of the Little Bighorn. Courage augmented by steady, decisive, and dynamic leadership was the key to victory. As the battles raged on, not one of the Indian leaders stood apart from the rest of the men, issuing orders. Instead, every one of them was in the thick of it, leading the way. This leadership by example turned the courage and skills of fighting men into an overwhelming force that the enemy could not match.

We know about the actions of Crazy Horse and Gall because they played prominent roles in one of the most storied battles in Lakota and American history. Yet several other lesser-known leaders performed just as effectively that day. All contributed to the final outcome: victory. And all were examples of the dynamic impact of leadership by example.

Leadership, of course, is not exclusive to the battle-field. Fortunately, we as human beings are engaged in a variety of more peaceful pursuits that are no less critical to achieving our goals. We all want to win, and we all want to achieve our desired objectives. To put it simply, we all want to be successful. A large part of success is having good leadership. Bad leadership, on the other hand, contributes more often than not to failure. Before we begin to make judgments about what leadership is good and what is bad, however, we must first define *leadership* itself.

In most dictionaries, a leader is defined as "one who leads," or "one who influences others." Interestingly, this definition does not mention *authority*, which seems to suggest that anyone who leads or influences others must do so by some other means. By extension, this also raises the question of whether anyone who is vested with authority in the hierarchy of any organization—

such as an administrator, CEO, mayor, governor, or even prime minister, premier, or president—is automatically a leader.

There is obviously a difference between issuing instructions, directives, and orders to accomplish an end, and influencing or inspiring others to act. Those who instruct, direct, and order others to do their bidding usually have the organizational authority to compel and, often, the power to punish if instructions, directives, and orders are not followed to their satisfaction. This begs the question: Are people responding to and following instructions, directives, and orders out of fear—either of failure or of punishment—or because they believe in the organization and its purpose?

It is entirely possible, of course, for anyone in a position of authority to be an effective leader. But first it is necessary to understand that leading is not the same as administering, managing, directing, or supervising. These acts are usually associated with rules, policies, budgets, procedures, manpower distribution, and other rather mundane but necessary organizational and operational processes. They are necessary because, in many of today's multilayered, multifaceted organizations and corporations, people need parameters within which to do their jobs. Boundaries for function and behavior are important to any organization that wants to be successful; but inspiration for the heart and the spirit should be important, too.

Because inspiration lends itself to the achievement of goals and objectives, inspirational leadership is as necessary for success as oxygen is for breathing. For precisely that reason, leadership is too important to be left solely to anyone elected or appointed to a position of authority, since being elected or appointed does not a leader make. No one has ever automatically acquired character or requisite qualities simply by election or appointment. Election and appointment may be a necessary part of the process, but neither imbues a person with benevolent omnipotence. Therefore, at the very least, a person who aspires to a position of authority should be carefully assessed. That includes his or her character and experience.

Perhaps the most important aspect of character is the ability to inspire by example, even if this means nothing more than telling the truth or doing what is right. Oftentimes this occurs in the places and situations we least expect, because leadership is a part of everyday life. Consider the child who sells lemonade and makes a few hundred dollars to send to the victims of a natural disaster or raises money to build a school for underprivileged children in Africa, or the man who has reported for work every day for thirty years without ever calling in sick. Society is defined by the everyday acts of ordinary people meeting their responsibilities and fulfilling their duties.

A quiet act of compassion or a singular demonstration of commitment may not be as dramatic as charging headlong into a hail of bullets on horseback in defense of home and country, but that doesn't diminish its power to inspire others. Selling lemonade or going to work every day is certainly not life threatening, but in terms of surviving and thriving from day to day, those kinds of acts are no less necessary. In their own way, they may be "the bravest things" a man, woman, or child can do. Without such examples, there are no standards for the rest of society to follow, nothing for people to emulate.

There will always be the Crazy Horses and Galls of the world. Over the ages, such individuals appear and rise to the challenge whenever there is a need. But if we think that dynamic leadership only occurs on the battleground, then we are denying ourselves the profound learning opportunities we are offered every day. Within many organizations and in every community there are ordinary people who rise to meet a need or to help achieve a seemingly simple goal. They may not capture the headlines or be noted in the history books, but these people nonetheless demonstrate the most effective model of leadership. They are showing the way by providing an example, and by doing so they also exemplify true leadership. Real leaders do not sit back and push people or papers around like pawns on a chessboard; real leaders say, "Follow me."

The actions of Crazy Horse and Gall during the Battle of the Little Bighorn contributed significantly to the Lakota and Northern Cheyenne victory. Those actions were not random, but were a consequence of their experience and status as military leaders. Even before that fateful day they had achieved leadership status as a result of their abilities and because Lakota society enabled the development of leaders—because strong leadership is essential to the survival and growth of any group.

Lakota society had existed and thrived for countless generations leading up to the Battle of the Little Bighorn, and not solely because of incredible luck. For any group of people to survive and thrive required strong social values and structure, as well as strong and consistent leadership for generation after generation. To avoid the mistaken conclusion that bad or failed Lakota leadership contributed to the eventual outcomes of the so-called clash of cultures with the Euro-Americans, we must examine the role of leadership in pre-European Lakota society. Second, we need to understand that several other factors affected the clash of cultures. Primary among those was the sheer, overwhelming number of new aggressors. In the mid-1800s the population of the United States was more than twenty million, while the Lakota numbered no more than twenty-five thousand. Furthermore, the technology developed by the Euro-Americans afforded them ballistic superiority. Add to all of that the mind-set of "Manifest Destiny" and the outcomes of Lakota–Euro-American interactions are understandable, perhaps even predictable.

In pre-reservation Lakota society, however—otherwise known as that period of several hundred years leading up to the late 1860s—leaders served in two broad and distinct categories: civilian and military. Boys grew up to be hunters to provide for their families and communities. They were also taught the skills to be fighting men, protectors of family, community, and nation. It was in the arena of military service and combat that young men had the opportunity to demonstrate the abilities and qualities that would set them apart as leadership material, to be considered by the community.

Since all males were groomed to function as warriors, every band had a ready military force, its size determined by the number of men in the community. It is safe to say that about 10 to 15 percent of the population of a village or band were able-bodied, full-fledged fighting men between the ages of eighteen and fifty. Therefore, in a village of two hundred people, for example, approximately twenty to thirty were warriors. It is interesting to note that when Crazy Horse surrendered to white authority at Fort Robinson in northwest Nebraska in May of 1877, his band numbered just over 900; approximately 130 of them—nearly 15 percent— were warriors. We can extrapolate, then, that if the Lakota, Dakota, and Nakota population in the mid-1800s was about 25,000, there were then 2,500 to 4,000 warriors.

But no matter how many warriors were in any given community or band, or in the nation overall, there was not a prescribed number of leadership positions. In modern American infantry units, the usual hierarchy from the top down is division, regiment, battalion, company, platoon, and squad. Squads are often further divided into fire teams. The larger the unit, the more leadership positions there are. A regiment, for example, has a regimental commander and his staff, and from there on down are the battalion commanders and their staffs, and then the company commanders, platoon commanders, squad leaders, and fire team leaders. There was no such structure among the Lakota, and therefore no prescribed number of leadership positions to be filled.

As a matter of fact, there was really no concept of authority in Lakota culture and no word for it. This is somewhat astounding so far as the operation of a military unit was concerned, because a Lakota leader could not rely on authority endorsed and supported by the community to compel a single man to follow him. Nevertheless, the Lakota did not lack for leaders. The absence of authority required that leaders rely on other factors, such as character and experience, to influence others to follow them.

The first step to military leadership was a man's performance in combat, which is arguably one of the most daunting experiences any person can face. For pre-reservation Indians, there was one intense, anticipatory moment every warrior-in-training faced: the moment during his very first combat action when he wrestled with the possibility of breaking and running. Once past that moment of truth, the next battle was easier to join thanks to the wisdom of experience. Yet even after a young man proved (mostly to himself) that he was capable of functioning in spite of his nervousness and fear, he still had to prove that he could physically face an enemy in close combat.

In that pre-reservation era, especially before the advent of firearms into the Lakota warrior's arsenal, most battles were fought face-to-face and toe-to-toe. Over time the actions and tendencies of up-and-coming warriors were observed by the older, more experienced men, especially the leaders. Combat leaders wanted fighting men who were not only physically skilled and strong, but who also possessed the qualities to perform within the unfettered chaos and violence of battle.

Crazy Horse set himself apart as a fighting man long before he ever became a candidate for leadership. He exhibited a consistent ability to remain calm and to function deliberately. As a matter of fact, many stories suggest that his first adult name, His Horse Stands in Sight, was a result of his actions in a few of his first encounters with Crow warriors. On more than one occasion he dismounted, walked several steps from his horse, and kneeled on one knee to take deliberate aim at the oncoming enemy. He also demonstrated early on that he was recklessly courageous, sometimes riding into enemy fire to rescue a wounded comrade, or leading a charge at the enemy as fast as his horse could gallop. It was these qualities that eventually drew other fighting men to Crazy Horse.

As a young man Crazy Horse was advised by his father to follow those warrior leaders who had good sense and many years of experience. Of course, a leader of fighting men does not survive long without a certain amount of good sense. But just as important, Crazy Horse's father (who was the second in his family to have the name His Crazy Horse) wanted his son to learn from someone with the right kind of experience and character. As a boy and young man, Crazy Horse had already been extensively mentored by a man named High Back Bone, or Hump, a Mniconju Lakota with a solid reputation. Hump taught him the skills of physical survival, weapons construction, and how to fight on foot as well as from the back of a horse. He also taught Crazy Horse the philosophy of being a warrior.

Lakota boys learned the necessary skills for hunting and warriorship through a successive, one-on-one mentoring process beginning with instruction from a father, uncle, grandfather, or close family friend. This process of teaching, guiding, and instructing one student at a time enabled the teacher to have an intense and profound influence; and through the experience the student learned that the power of experience and character was the greatest influence any man could wield. Therefore, there was no need to compel with authority.

No matter the depth of any man's experience as a leader of fighting men, or the strength of his character, he was still aware that every other fighting man had the right of free choice. That is, every individual warrior could choose whether or not to follow any leader. Free choice was not exclusive to fighting men, however. In Lakota society, free choice was paramount and every man and woman had that right.

The choice to follow any leader of fighting men was entirely subjective, of course. Choices were based on family ties, politics, friendship, reputation, or the mission. Generally speaking, a military leader announced that he was undertaking a particular mission and issued invitations to fighting men to join him. Frequently, leaders would issue invitations only to particular individuals. The response depended on the stature and reputation of the man issuing the call, as well as his record as a leader.

To find an example of warriors responding to the reputation, experience, and character of a leader, we must turn once again to an event in Lakota history—ten years before the Battle of the Little Bighorn, to an event known as the Battle of the Hundred in the Hand. To Euro-Americans it is the Fetterman Battle (or Massacre) of December 21, 1866.

After the United States ignored its own assurances not to enter Lakota territory, establish roads, or build forts and outposts without Lakota permission, the die was cast for continuous conflict along a route known to history as the Bozeman Trail. The trail served as a quick route to the goldfields west of Virginia City, Montana Territory, from south-central Wyoming Territory. To protect gold seekers traveling to their fortunes, three forts were built along the trail—Fort Reno near Kaycee, Wyoming; Fort Philip Kearny between Buffalo and Sheridan, Wyoming; and Fort C. F. Smith near Hardin, Montana. All three outposts were bones of contention for the Lakota, but Fort Philip Kearny was especially problematic.

Because U.S. soldiers were always better armed with plenty of ammunition, the Lakota knew that other battle tactics had to be used in order to negate their numerical superiority and firepower. So they relied on their superior abilities as cavalry and the age-old tactic of ambush. But the seven hundred soldiers inside Fort Philip Kearny essentially refused to come out for a protracted engagement. Though the Lakota (and Northern Cheyenne) did manage to lure small units miles beyond the protective walls of the fort on several occasions, the ambushes were spoiled by impatient and overzealous young warriors who fired prematurely.

After one such debacle in early December 1866, the older men severely disciplined the offending young warriors and then made a fateful decision. They would make another attempt at luring the soldiers into an ambush by using a small number of decoy warriors. If the decoys were successful in luring soldiers out of the fort, they would fall into a trap of four to five hundred warriors waiting in ambush. But the trap was four miles from the fort—four miles of rough, uneven, and frozen terrain covered with ice and snow.

The old men leaders shrewdly knew that the soldiers would be more likely to pursue a small group of warriors, so they decided that there should be no more than ten decoys. The most critical part of the equation, however, was to pick a leader of the decoys whose experience and reputation would be strong enough to influence nine other capable men to follow according to plan. They selected Crazy Horse, and allowed him to choose the rest of the men for the job.

Word spread among the Lakota, Northern Cheyenne, and Arapaho warriors that Crazy Horse would lead a team of decoys to lure soldiers into an ambush. Hundreds of fighting men volunteered to ride with him, not only because of the dangerous mission but because they knew Crazy Horse. Although he was only in his early twenties at the time, his actions on the battlefield in several major campaigns were well known. He had earned more battle honors at that point in his life than many men did in an entire lifetime. He was also familiar with the experience level of many of his contemporaries. By the afternoon and evening of December 20, he had picked his fellow decoys—all of whom were young or still in their prime, with superior skills as horsemen and warriors.

On the bitter cold morning of December 21, 1866 (thirty degrees below zero, according to thermometers in the fort), a wood train rolled out from Philip Kearny and headed west toward the foothills. A group of warriors attacked it, and subsequently eighty soldiers were deployed from the fort to rescue the wood detail, including several wagons, civilian workers, and a military escort. Crazy Horse attacked the rescue column before it reached the wood detail and turned it north.

The soldiers chased Crazy Horse and his decoys for just over four miles, directly into the trap. The decoys led the soldiers past the waiting ambushers and signaled the hidden warriors, who quickly surrounded the soldiers. The ensuing, hard-fought battle probably lasted less than an hour and every soldier was killed.

The brave and cunning actions of the young Crazy Horse lent greatly to the victory that day in the Battle of the Hundred in the Hand—indeed, they were the reason the battle had occurred at all. Yet everyone had played an important part in the events that unfolded: His elders knew that Crazy Horse would be a leader in the not-too-distant future because of his experience and character, two important factors to which everyone responded. The decoy warriors who participated in the all-important ruse to lure the soldiers performed to the level of their own skills and experience, and exhibited the kind of character that wins battles. Still, it is safe to say that some, if not most, of them performed above and beyond the call of duty simply because of the reputation and actions of the man leading them. That kind of well-earned respect characterized leadership in Lakota society and allowed them to fulfill a critical purpose or achieve a difficult objective without the weight of authority.

It is widely assumed by those who know—or think they know—the story of Crazy Horse that he became a leader only because of his exploits on the battlefield. Yet while it is true that he certainly brought attention to himself through his bravery, especially when he placed himself in harm's way to turn the tide of battle or go to the aid of a fellow warrior, his reputation and success as a leader also came from his ability to stay calm under the most difficult of circumstances. The rationale was that if a man could prove his mettle on the ground of combat while facing the prospect of injury and death, he probably had what it took to face the tough decisions of everyday life.

Every Lakota village in pre-reservation days was a small town, and usually many of the people in one village or community were related by blood or marriage. Therefore, everyone knew about everyone else. Adults had the opportunity to watch all the children in the community as they grew and matured. The positive aspect of such scrutiny was that people knew intimately the family background and character of each new generation. It was, therefore, not surprising to most people that young Crazy Horse demonstrated a sincere concern for the welfare of others; his parents taught him those values as he was growing up, and as a teenager he would often hunt and bring home fresh meat for elderly people and widows. So, while his battlefield exploits drew the attention and loyalty of other fighting men (and the focus of non-Indian historians), his quiet nature and compassion endeared him to everyone else.

In Lakota social structure the number of leaders was not as important as the qualities a leader possessed. Or as one Lakota elder put it, "One man with good character is better than ten who have none." Men such as Gall, Sitting Bull, and Crazy Horse epitomized the Lakota ideal of leadership. They accomplished this not only through their bravery or powers of persuasion, but most importantly through the depth of their character.

THE FIRST PRINCIPLE: KNOW YOURSELF

The best that any of us can do is face life with our strengths and weaknesses—but to do so we must be brutally honest with ourselves about both. Anything less is misleading at best, and potentially dangerous.

Skills and abilities not applied consistently become dull or rusty over time. Yet while some things may be lost or diminished, we learn new skills, develop new abilities, and gain experience. We are all works in progress. As time goes on we should become more and more able to deal with life's challenges. Therefore, because things change, self-awareness must be a constant discipline.

Never in our personal or professional lives will we come to a point where we have learned it all. While the rapid pace of technology today keeps us constantly on the line between mastery and obsolescence, the principle of continuous personal and professional development is not new. Even in the pre-reservation period, Lakota archers worked constantly to hone their abilities and instincts. Bows and arrows were the premier weapons for hundreds, if not thousands, of years. Survival in every sense of the word depended on the skills and commitment of the males who fulfilled the societal roles of protectors and providers—the warriors and hunters. Expertise with the bow and arrow defended against enemies and provided food and shelter. Skills with those weapons were never allowed to diminish. Therefore, the most highly skilled archers were males fifty years of age and older. As a matter of fact, a popular sentiment was that *a man would only stop improving with a bow on the day he died.*

As we continue to develop skills and gain experience, we should also never stop being honest with ourselves about our strengths and weaknesses. While archery may no longer be considered a vital daily skill, one strength we must have in common with the pre-reservation Lakota is learning to handle increasing types and degrees of responsibility.

While Crazy Horse lived to his mid-thirties, which may seem like a very short life in contemporary terms, for nearly fifteen of those years he was responsible for the safety and welfare of other people beyond his own family. He learned early on that the greater part of being a leader was responsibility. He also learned that the achievement of glory did nothing to diminish the responsibility, or make it easier to meet. But because the responsibility had to be fulfilled, Crazy Horse turned to the first tools at his disposal: his own abilities, capabilities, experience, and character.

From all indications, Crazy Horse did not aspire to leadership. In his early days as an unproven and inexperienced would-be warrior, he had the same training and physical skills as other young men. His first objective—like that of any other young man of the time—was not to lose his nerve. Like many, many others who faced that moment of truth on the battlefield, Crazy Horse was immensely relieved as he stood his ground. Of course, it was not long before he proved to himself and to other fighting men that he was more than equal to the task of being a warrior.

Because combat presented an opportunity to prove one's character if one had aspirations toward leadership, it was not unusual for Lakota fighting men to attempt to distinguish themselves as warriors. But Crazy Horse was honest and aware of his own inexperience, so he did the responsible thing and followed the lead of the experienced men, such as his mentor High Back Bone, and Spotted Tail, his uncle by marriage. He did not intend to set himself apart with attention-grabbing exploits on the battlefield. But in reacting to the flow of battle with bravery and skill, he did exactly that on more than one occasion.

The first characteristic that other men immediately noticed in Crazy Horse was his steadiness under pressure. On one notable expedition against the Crow, more than two hundred men followed Red Cloud's banner because of his position within a highly influential family. But one contingent including Crazy Horse, High Back Bone, and Crazy Horse's younger brother Little Hawk attracted significant attention and a strong following. This fact did not go unnoticed by Red Cloud. Leadership, in a real sense, came to Crazy Horse.

Most people who accomplish the extraordinary or set themselves apart do not actually set out to do so. There is no special school for the training of heroes except for life itself. Crazy Horse was the beneficiary of a teaching and mentoring process used and refined over many generations. That process not only ensured physical survival, but also the survival of the culture. Children gained skills and knowledge necessary to procure the basic necessities of food, shelter, clothing, and security. But perhaps more important, they were inculcated with the foundations of their culture so that it would survive from one generation to the next.

We know from history that Crazy Horse responded to the challenges and responsibilities of leadership, but what is less obvious—or less often the subject of popular imagination—are how and why he was able to respond the way he did. Cultures around the world recite the deeds of their heroes but have a tendency to overlook the basis, cause, or motivation for those deeds. What made Crazy Horse a dynamic leader is, in many ways, just as important as his record as a warrior. To understand what made him a legend, we must look at the process and the culture that forged him into a man.

Within the context of cultural survival, Lakota men and women had separate but equally critical societal roles. Dwelling and family were the responsibility of women. They sewed buffalo hides together to make the outer covering and inner winter linings of the dwelling, constructed much of the furniture used by all members of the family, and made clothing, among many other never-ending chores. Consequently, the dwelling and everything in it, except for her husband's personal possessions, was the woman's property.

While the construction and maintenance of the dwelling was important, the most critical role for women was raising the children and nurturing the family. If families were strong, then the community—the *tiyospaye*—was strong. And if communities were strong, then the nation was strong. In this role, women were the foundation of Lakota culture.

No matter what else they became in life, Lakota males were expected to fulfill the dual roles of provider and protector, or hunter and warrior. As hunters, men procured the basic necessities for food, shelter, and clothing. Perhaps as much as 70 percent of their time was spent hunting for fresh meat—and hides, to be used for clothing and a variety of other household and personal items. In most instances this meant traveling for days away from the village. As warriors, on the other hand, they had the responsibility to protect family, community, and nation. The standing Lakota military force was constantly on alert, capable of engaging any enemy in an instant.

All of the skills and most of the weapons used by hunters and warriors were interchangeable, and that is where their lessons began. Almost always, two things became a constant part of a boy's life: a bow and a horse. It was the intent of the teacher that shooting the bow and riding the horse would become second nature, because the two skills would one day be intertwined for the hunter and warrior. While it was necessary for a boy to gain more than average proficiency with the bow, it was expected that his proficiency not decrease when he was on the back of a moving horse.

As he became stronger and more coordinated, the Lakota boy was introduced to other weapons, such as the war club and lance. Both were used in close combat, but a much longer version of the war lance was also used in buffalo hunting. Here again, skill on horseback was essential, as the buffalo hunters approached their prey not unlike medieval knights, quartering in from the rear of the animal with a seven-foot lance.

Practice was the key to proficiency and to advancing through the benchmarks of the different skill levels. As an archer, for example, the boy was expected to be able to hit a grasshopper on the fly. He was also expected to hit both a stationary and a moving target from the back of a galloping horse. Overall, it was not uncommon for boys in their mid-teens to launch arrows at the rate of twelve to fifteen per minute.

Physical skills such as horsemanship, marksmanship, and hand-to-hand fighting could be easily assessed. Ancillary skills such as tracking and survival were just as critical. Yet because the training was one-on-one, boys and young men did not compete against one another in any organized manner. In this way, leaders were distinguished by their own abilities rather than through peer pressure.

Without a doubt, the roles for both men and women were critical to the stability, strength, and survival of the Lakota culture. But one role often overlooked was just as important as any other: that of the teacher and mentor. Women were the first teachers of all children. Thereafter they taught their daughters and granddaughters to fulfill their societal roles as mothers, nurturers, and homemakers. Likewise, boys and young men were taught by their fathers, uncles, and grandfathers to be hunters and warriors. The strength of the educative process was that it never included anyone who was totally separate from the family. If the teacher and mentor was not a relative, then he or she was a close friend. It was easier to establish a bond and a trust with an adult the child knew and admired or respected. In the same way, it was easier for the teacher-mentor to remain committed to the development of a son, grandson, daughter, granddaughter, niece, or nephew, or the child of a friend.

There was another positive consequence to this process, beyond the obvious one that boys and girls became responsible young men and women aware of their place in Lakota society. At some point during adolescence, most young people came to the realization that there was little they could hide from the people around them, because, as in most small and close-knit communities, everyone knew everyone else. If a young person did not come to this realization on his or her own, then parents, grandparents, or someone else in the extended family was certain to tell them! It was a critical and necessary lesson in honest self-awareness. That lesson was just as valuable as all the others that were learned, especially for any young man who aspired to be a leader.

If we are honest with ourselves, we sooner or later realize that no matter what image we try to project to the rest of the world, we can only act and function from what we truly are. In a contemporary example, let's say that Ralph wants to impress John and, therefore, tells John that he is a pilot. That "truth" about Ralph exists in John's mind. Then an urgent business situation arises and John asks Ralph to fly him to a town five hundred miles away. Ralph now has two choices: He may confess that he is not a pilot, or he might make up an excuse to avoid revealing his lie. But he will have learned that being honest with other people means also being honest with himself. Sadly, in some instances, some of us learn that lesson later rather than sooner. Furthermore, we often allow the perceptions of others to get in the way of being our authentic selves.

A Lakota story for children offers a lesson in how we can be affected by what others think of us. The protagonist of this story, and others like it, is always Trickster. His Lakota name is Iktomi. And Iktomi has an unfortunate habit of learning the hard way.

Over a period of several days Iktomi sees his face reflected on the surface of a pond. One day there is bright sunshine, and the next there is wind. On the third day there are heavy clouds, and on the last day it rains. He likes what he sees, of course, when the pond is calm and the sun is shining. But under the other conditions, his reflection is changed, becoming dark and distorted and not very flattering at all. Iktomi rationalizes that those reflections are not him.

The story is obviously a metaphor for the perceptions other people have of us, which are often different from how we perceive ourselves. The moral of the story is that while others' images and perceptions are only part of the reality of who and what we are, they can also prevent our own self-perception from getting out of hand.

Like Iktomi, we are frequently confronted with other people's perceptions of us in our personal and professional lives. And also like Iktomi, we might be flattered by positive perceptions and hurt by others, or we might choose to ignore them altogether. If we are not careful we may allow our self-awareness to be skewed or enhanced beyond any semblance of reality—and that can also affect our self-esteem. The moral for us, then, is that we should know ourselves best, and realistically.

Crazy Horse's self-knowledge began with his mother. Rattling Blanket Woman was aware that her child's complexion and hair were lighter than usual. While it was not unheard of among the Lakota people to have brown hair and light skin, it was just unusual enough to set someone apart, especially a boy. Rattling Blanket Woman knew that her son would be teased, and, to lessen the sting of it, she gave him the childhood name Jiji, or Light Haired One. Although the name did not stop other children from teasing him, it did teach the boy to accept himself as he was.

In essence, Crazy Horse's birth mother turned an anomaly into a source of strength for her son. As an adult he learned that brown hair and light skin were minor issues compared to character, common sense, and a list of other issues for which he was consistently judged. But having experienced and endured ridicule as a child, he learned that realistic self-awareness could not deter ridicule or criticism, but it could become a source of strength if he accepted himself for what he was. It was not just his childhood name, however, that offered a life lesson.

Crazy Horse, like all Lakota children in pre-reservation days, grew up under the care, guidance, and scrutiny of practically every adult in the village. Beyond his parents, grandparents, aunts, and uncles, there were other adults who had something to offer. By the time he reached young manhood, Crazy Horse, then still known as Light Hair, was a known entity. More important, his growth and development as an individual were supported and affected by people who genuinely cared about him. In other words, Crazy Horse was a child of the village.

Like other boys in the village, his training as a hunter and warrior started around the age of five. Because his father, the second man in his family to have the name Crazy Horse, was a healer or medicine man, most of his time was devoted to his patients. His brothers, Crazy Horse's uncles, stepped in to take the boy under their wings, becoming his first instructors. Later, High Back Bone, or Hump, became the boy's teacher. Hump and the boy formed a friendship that endured until Hump was killed in a fight with Shoshone Indians when Crazy Horse was in his late twenties.

The relationship between teacher and student was the foundation for realistic self-awareness. For the teacher to be effective, he had to know the student's strengths and weaknesses and tailor the lessons accordingly. The general plan, of course, was to eliminate the weaknesses and build on the strengths. As the relationship developed, the teacher spoke honestly to his student about both. That honesty, the student sooner or later realized, was necessary for him to learn his lessons and do what his teacher expected of him. Therefore, in addition to the physical skills and abilities he learned and improved, the boy had to learn to look at himself realistically.

Lessons were not easy and became more difficult as the boy grew older. He was constantly pushed to the limits of patience, strength, and endurance and challenged physically, mentally, and emotionally. While there was praise for his success, there was also honest assessment of his failures. When the teacher was satisfied that the student had learned and mastered all the necessary skills to be an adequate hunter and warrior, he was allowed to hunt on his own and to accompany warriors on military patrols.

As mentioned before, another consequence of the long training and mentoring process was that each boy's family, teachers, and mentors knew the young man's strengths and weaknesses as well as he did. This was an effective deterrent to false pride. Because most of the people in the village or community knew each boy, they also knew when he attempted to embellish something about his skills and abilities. Someone, including himself, was always available to steer him back to the path of realistic self-awareness.

Throughout Crazy Horse's life the village was a source of strength, motivation, and inspiration. Unfortunately, the concept of village has weakened in recent generations and its place in American society has all but disappeared. Although the concept that "it takes a village to raise a child" has been recently "discovered" as an appealing catchphrase, the village experience no longer exists in American society, making it difficult to functionally apply the concept. To begin with, the foundation of the nuclear family is geographically splintered due to various factors. Primary among these, of course, are career and work.

In pre-reservation days the community remained intact generation after generation because families did not move away. The most frequent changes occurred as a result of marriage. It was the young man who left his family to become part of his wife's, literally moving next door to his wife's parents into a new lodge provided by the women in his wife's family. When an entire family did move into a village, they were usually given a spot next to their relatives.

Since the Lakota were a nomadic hunting society, villages relocated often, especially from spring to autumn. Still, the basic layout of any village did not change no matter where it stood. More important, the basic social function and interaction continued without interruption. Parents, grandparents, and friends were always nearby and available. For sons that had married into families in other villages, they were not so isolated from one another that distance precluded regular visits.

All in all, the village remained intact and consistently available as a viable source of support.

If there is one predictable factor about American society and Western societies in general today, it is that they are in constant flux. Furthermore, progress or change in one specific sector projects the illusion that everything is changing. Technology is the primary illusionist, due mainly to rapid and sensational changes to the things in our lives—automobiles, computers, and telephones, for example—and the advent of new technology nearly every day. A direct and unfortunate consequence is that the less-tangible aspects of community and society—those lacking physical characteristics or a discernible dollar value—such as respect, devotion, courtesy, and family values, have been ignored, overlooked, disregarded, and even discarded. The function of the village, therefore, has not only been dramatically altered but also woefully outpaced by rapid technological change. Whether we are aware of it or not, we as individuals are diminished by the demise of the village in our modern society, because we can no longer rely on the strength of the village to support and complement our efforts or validate our sense of identity.

Years after the nomadic hunting lifestyle had ended for the Lakota, Black Elk, a contemporary of Crazy Horse, commented on the growth of Lakota boys into men:

The Washicus have put us in these square boxes,
our power is gone and we are dying, for the
power is not in us any more. You can look at our
boys and see how it is with us. When we were
living by the power of the circle in the way we
should, boys were men at the age of twelve or
thirteen. But now it takes them much longer to
mature.

Black Elk was one of those boys who "were men at the age of twelve or thirteen." They knew firsthand that they were capable of surviving on their own in the wilderness and helped provide for their families with their hunting skills. Part of the ability to survive was self-sufficiency.

In Lakota society, everything that was used, worn, or consumed was hunted, collected, prepared, and made by someone. By the age of twelve, boys had a basic knowledge of crafting techniques to make weapons; and under the tutelage of older men, they perfected their skills by making their own bows and arrows, knives, war clubs, and lances, as well as all the tools and accoutrements they would need to take into the field as hunters and warriors. Once a young man improved the skills to craft his own weapons, he had fulfilled the last requirement to be self-sufficient. Yet there was still another dimension that was as critical to the young would-be hunter-warrior as physical skills and self-sufficiency.

Attitude had been carefully developed and instilled by the fathers, grandfathers, uncles, relatives, and friends of the family, who had taken their turns at teaching and mentoring a boy and guided him along the path to becoming a hunter and warrior. The lessons had been as comprehensive and as difficult as the teacher-mentor could make them because the responsibility and duty to be a provider and protector was not easy. Consequently, by the age of sixteen to eighteen, a young man already had considerable experience helping his father as a hunter. He was also prepared and eager to take his place as a full-fledged fighting man. He had been allowed to accompany experienced warriors in the field to observe and participate to the extent that the older men deemed was acceptable and necessary.

At every step along the way, interspersed among the lessons, practice, and excursions, the teacher-mentor had developed the mind-set of the hunter-warrior with a mechanism just as necessary and effective as the physical aspects of training: stories of men who had walked the trail before them. He learned that he had a legacy of successes and failures, battles won and lost, and strengths and weaknesses of relatives and ancestors who left examples for him to emulate or avoid. The hero stories were about men who had really lived, and not about mythical characters with adventures and abilities beyond those of real people. The boys and young men also listened to each teacher-mentor's own experiences as a warrior, as well as the opinions he had formed and the philosophies he had followed.

Eventually, the young man's thinking would be shaped by his own experiences, but it was built upon a foundation that was supported by the generations. Even as an untested fighting man, he learned that his family, community, and nation expected him to be fully committed to his calling. And the moment he stepped onto the field, he dedicated himself to living up to those expectations.

Of course, the individual accomplishments of Lakota fighting men varied widely, but most fulfilled the role of warrior to the best of their abilities. It is probably safe to say that most of them did not want to be leaders, but by the same token most of them were devoted to their families and were an integral part of their communities. That the Lakota, Dakota, and Nakota nation thrived and grew in population and territory after their arrival on the northern plains can be attributed largely to the commitment, dedication, and solidarity of the warrior culture within the nation.

Because circumstances have altered the lifestyle of the Lakota, Dakota, and Nakota nation, the hunter-warrior is part of the past. Though his time-honored traditions and skills are no longer relevant to daily life, his commitment and dedication to family, community, and nation are still every bit as necessary. Today the training of the hunter-warrior in pre-reservation Lakota society can be seen as an object lesson.

Because the survival of the family, the community, and the nation depended on everyone fulfilling their societal roles, the village mentored each young hunter-warrior in the skills and values he would need to fulfill his calling. Yet while the system of preparing young men to be providers and protectors was the same across the culture, what young men did after attaining those basic skills was up to them.

Any group or society meets its needs when everyone agrees on the objective and works together toward its achievement. The chances for success, however, are greatly increased when a good leader provides effective input and direction. Lakota society long ago recognized that good leadership was a necessity in any endeavor. Because they knew that adversity was the best proving ground for the character of up-and-coming leaders, each young man who set foot on the warpath was as thoroughly trained as the previous generations of warriors could train him. That meant that the skills and abilities of the warrior would be less of an issue when a man was considered for or aspired to leadership. But if skill alone did not a leader make, then which qualities were considered to be critical in assessing any man's fitness for leadership? The answer is both logical and profound: character and experience. And both of these depended upon an honest self-awareness.

A man's understanding of his own skills and abilities was the basis for his sense of confidence and positive self-esteem—or the lack of both. But the society that had shaped him into a hunter and warrior also made it virtually impossible for him to misrepresent himself. Communities were small, two hundred to five hundred people, and smaller in the winter. While warfare allowed a man to draw attention to himself through his deeds, those deeds had to be verified by others who were there.

The Lakota had a custom called *waktoglakapi,* meaning "to tell of one's victories." It was an opportunity for a warrior to publicly recount a deed in battle, as long as witnesses could attest to it. Many men followed the tradition, but some did not. Crazy Horse was one of the latter. His deeds were described by others who had seen him in action. He disdained the ceremony because he was shy, but also because he was genuinely humble.

A man's reputation and conduct as a fighter was a matter of public record, even though he might not have participated in the *waktoglakapi*. There was no documentation, of course, but there was general knowledge, because information was shared and stories circulated, especially about notable and spectacular exploits. If any man had aspirations to leadership, that record was unalterable. Today the situation is somewhat similar, because the résumés of public officials elected, appointed, or hired, are a matter of public record, although it is incumbent upon the community to seek and obtain that information. But there is one notable exception: Education and experience are important requirements, and for positions of responsibility and authority it is necessary to establish a positive track record of achievement. This is all well and good, but even the most solid and impeccable résumé cannot necessarily provide a true picture of a person's character.

While there are several ways in which character is developed, it is most often revealed in difficult, critical, and stressful situations. At the end of the day, though, no matter who and what we are or what station we hold in life, we as individuals are the first keepers of the truth when it comes to knowing about ourselves.

An alarming aspect of the 2007–2008 campaign for president in the United States had to do with the résumés of the myriad candidates. The voting public, responding to a poll in the summer of 2007, did not think to rate experience high on the scale as a major factor in determining qualifications for office. Obviously, only an incumbent running for a second term has experience as president. The next best qualifier, however, is experience as a sensible, compassionate, and selfless leader. What is most alarming about the poll results is the apparently low expectations of voters and their general lack of interest in such significant indicators of leadership potential.

In this day and age, because America is not one big village, we are not able to witness the rise and development of all those among us who would be leaders. According to Joel Garreau, author of *The Nine Nations of North America*, we are a compilation of regional societies arranged by geography, ethnicity, values, and class, spilling over into Mexico and Canada. Because our population is more than 300 million, even the best-known leader in any field is, for the most part, one of many faces in the crowd. Most of us have no true and substantive information, not to mention first-hand knowledge, about any one of those faces with which to determine prospective leaders' qualifications. There is no true "child of the village" in whom we can unhesitatingly put our trust, because trust is a relationship based on awareness and consistent performance to earn and hold that trust. Without the close scrutiny of the village—be it the American people or the hiring bodies of a particular industry—it is next to impossible to separate fact from fiction when a candidate represents him- or herself to the public.

In the political arena, presidential candidates arise from the masses every four years to tout their own potential as leader of the United States. Voters are assailed with hype about issues and promises to fix what is broken, and we are sucked into the promise of bigger and better. Come election day, we vote largely on the hope that one candidate will actually keep his or her promises. Yet we forget to look at how many promises they have kept, or failed to keep, as senator, governor, mayor, or whatever they were before they zeroed in on the prize of being president. The tragedy is that in the cacophony of hype and promises, real and relevant experience is not given enough consideration. That is not to say that we should expect our candidates to be perfect, but that we must act on our right to accurate information.

One obstacle to this, however, is that there is a double-edged sword in the process itself: A winning candidate must have both the requisite experience to do the job well and experience as a successful politician. Politics is the downside for many reasons. The ability to thrive as a politician is not always honed along the high road of ethics. A successful politician is skilled in the art of give-and-take, but much too frequently basic ethical values are given away in return for influence or dollars poured into campaign coffers. When that is the case, those politicians must then serve a few whose bottom line is more important than the needs, wishes, and welfare of the many. Almost without exception this unfortunate reality of politics consistently reveals the greatest shortcoming of politicians: the lack of character.

The harshest measure of any society is a lack of character in its leaders. But the even sadder consequence is the effect a leader's lack of character has on society. Of course, the most frequent victims are the poor and disaffected, the underserved, the voiceless and powerless—those who depend on the character of leaders to bring comfort from their afflictions and give them a voice.

Perhaps the ways in which we choose our leaders today are too complicated and ponderous, or too elitist, to allow the average person to gauge the true worth and qualifications of anyone who seeks our vote. Because that process heavily favors politics and the politician, there will likely not be any changes in the foreseeable future. So perhaps one way to sift through the hype is for voters to look first and longest at what any candidate has done and pay no heed to mere words about what they say they have done or who they say they are. Anyone can put together a résumé to show his or her good or strongest side, but actions have always spoken louder than words. Mandatory, publicly disclosed background checks by a neutral body may be the only way to force a candidate to truly know and represent him- or herself factually. Barring this, the onus is on us as individuals to know our potential leaders as best we can. Anyone who votes to decrease the tax liability for millionaires and billionaires, for example, yet votes against pay raises for young men and women whose military wage is barely above the poverty line has revealed a lack of character. Ultimately, character and integrity often come down to a basic willingness to make personal sacrifices for the greater good.

It is said that sometime before 1876 a young Lakota man broke away from the government agencies near Fort Robinson, in what is now northwestern Nebraska. Many Lakota people were already living on reservations by then, languishing on agencies under the control of the U.S. government's Bureau of Indian Affairs. The young man could no longer stand the restricted life and yearned for freedom, so he journeyed north, riding his only horse and carrying hardly any other possessions. He found Crazy Horse's village in the Powder River region, in what is now north central Wyoming. There he made his plea to the famed leader, asking to join him.

Crazy Horse asserted that the young man was welcome, so long as he was willing to perform a task:

He was to kill his horse. The young man protested because it was practically his only possession. So, unable to carry out the request, he sadly turned around and headed back toward the agency. Puzzled by the incident, one of Crazy Horse's friends wanted to know why he had made such a difficult request of the young man. Crazy Horse assured his friend that he certainly would have stopped the young man from actually killing the horse. Furthermore, if the young man had indicated a willingness to comply, he would have also made a gift of a horse from his own herd. The important thing, Crazy Horse pointed out, was that the young man would be willing to sacrifice everything he had to be part of the village. At the time, Crazy Horse's band of nearly a thousand people, and Sitting Bull's people farther to the northeast, were the last of the free Lakota. It was a difficult time and required the people to make sacrifices for one another for the sake of survival. According to Crazy Horse, the young man's inability to make that sacrifice indicated a weakness in his character. That kind of weakness was a threat to the entire community.

Lack of character results in a weak leader, and a weak leader is a threat to the survival of those to whom he or she is responsible, if and when that lack causes ineffective or bad leadership. When that occurs, should that person be considered less than us, the individual members of the community? Or is his or her stumble simply a reflection of the rest of us?

When officials do their jobs at least adequately, there is usually some degree of disappointment on our part, because we expect more. When they make mistakes, some of us feel more than a little disappointment. We do expect much from our leaders. But is it fair to hold them to a higher standard than we expect of ourselves?

Leaders of organizations, companies, and corporations should realize that their basic ethical responsibility is to reflect the values of the people they lead, and hold themselves to a higher standard in regard to value and character. Because individuals make up the community, group, or organization, our values and character shape those of the whole. We can expect that our leaders—be they pastors, company executives, or elected officials—reflect the core of what we bring to the community, the group, or the organization. That means that the responsibility is also on us to uphold our own highest standards.

As individuals, we must know ourselves better than anyone else can. That is to say that we should know ourselves honestly. That is the first challenge of leadership.

There are ways and means by which anyone can meet this challenge. Mentorship was a proven component in Lakota society. While it may not be a societal norm today, it can still be an effective tool for anyone to develop individual skills and character. Even without the village structure or worldview, there are many people in all of our lives who have the life experiences to serve as mentors.

Although the right of individual choice was paramount in Lakota society, through honest self-awareness the people learned that their survival, identity, and welfare were provided and enabled by the village, community, and nation. Therefore, individuals were not hesitant to dedicate themselves to the common good.

Instead of depending on the benevolence of a single leader, we must work together to achieve our goals. When this happens, leaders can do no less. Yes, they have a choice to reflect the attitudes and effort of the community and be empowered by it, or to oppose it with inaction. But a leader who reflects the values and efforts of his or her community cannot take advantage of its weaknesses. One who does not reflect those values, on the other hand, may not hold on to the power of leadership for long.

In past Lakota society, the community had a definite sense of identity and values that made it cohesive and strong. Those who became leaders developed their identity from the community itself. This left little room or opportunity for leaders to drift away from their root values. Because that village dynamic is no longer a part of modern society, we as individuals are not children of the village in the same way that Crazy Horse was. But the core values of communities, organizations, and companies are still established by the individuals who are their citizens, members, and employees. For the most part, those values reflect the best and most positive aspects of the group.

When the individuals who make up a community, organization, or company consistently practice those positive values, it is realistic to expect that their leaders will do the same. But the group must know itself honestly so that its leaders are motivated to do the same. In that way, the "village" can help its leaders to meet the first challenge of leadership.

THE SECOND PRINCIPLE: KNOW YOUR FRIENDS

Leaders cannot do everything. More to the point, they cannot do anything alone. The word *leader* implies that there are others—those who need to be led—involved. In a broad sense, anyone not leading is following. The leader's first task is to identify those people who are committed to a goal and have the necessary skills and abilities to help achieve it, and then motivate them to follow. The trick is how.

A wily army sergeant once assembled a squad of soldiers and announced that he had a very special assignment, then asked if any of them happened to be musicians. Several soldiers raised their hands, thinking they had latched on to easy duty in the regimental band. Leading his volunteers to a building on the far side of the base, the sergeant showed them a five-hundred-pound grand piano that had to be moved to the general's house.

Authority can be a wonderful thing, but to depend on it first and always—either as a leader or a follower—is to disenfranchise the leader-follower dynamic. Unhealthy dependence on authority does not enable the leader to assess the abilities, commitment, or character of the followers. As necessary as authority may be, it is not the backbone of leadership.

Crazy Horse had many admirers and hundreds of loyal followers. In May 1877, nearly a thousand people, young and old, followed Crazy Horse to an uncertain and unpredictable situation at Fort Robinson, Nebraska, where he surrendered to Euro-American authority. They followed him, essentially placing their day-to-day welfare into the hands of people they despised, because they knew what kind of a man and leader he was. Yet the time had come when Crazy Horse realized that surrender was necessary for their survival. The people trusted him and, likewise, Crazy Horse trusted the people. He knew their values, what they were capable of, and who they were. Most important, they had faced and endured many hardships together. This relationship epitomizes the second philosophy of leadership that emerges from Crazy Horse's life: Know your friends.

Good leadership is certainly not exclusive to one culture or one group of people. Neither are opportunities for character-building life lessons.

Once a man came to a village called Songhai and took up residence in a rented house. He was neither plain nor handsome, but he had a quick and easy smile and struck up conversations easily. His most noticeable feature was a thin scar that ran from above his right eyebrow to the right corner of his mouth. Also hard to miss was the slight limp in his step. Most of all, he carried himself with an air of competence. When asked, he replied that his name was Fox, late of the army, retiring after years as the captain of a company of mounted lancers.

Captain Fox frequented the town square, where the old men of the village gathered to play cards and chess, and to smoke their pipes and talk. He politely hung back until he was invited into a conversation, and was always respectful. One day he revealed that he was thinking of leading an expedition across the most forbidding corner of the continent, called the Shadow Lands—a region that was comprised of a scorching desert, extremely high, snow-capped mountains, and a steamy jungle. Though many had tried, no one man or group of men had ever successfully

traversed it. As a matter of fact, the few who dared
had not lived to tell about their adventures.

"One man cannot do it alone," the old men told him.
"You will need a mountain climber, and a man who
knows the desert, and one who knows the jungle. You
will also need a leader who knows their weaknesses as
well as their strengths."

Captain Fox listened to the old men and took their
advice to heart. He had picked the village of Songhai
because it was at a crossroads. Many people passed
through it on their way to the far corners of the land.
As the days and weeks passed, Fox frequented the
village square and simply listened and carefully
observed the colorful travelers. Now and then he
would approach one and invite him to share a smoke
or a pint of bitter and engage in a bit of conversation.
To any other observer, it would seem that Fox was
simply being friendly. But after such encounters,
Captain Fox would settle down on a bench in the
village square and carefully make notes in his
journal. He was seen to frequently study the pages of
notes he had compiled. He also frequently asked the

old men in the square if they had heard of this person or that. Sometimes they had and Fox would probe with questions. As time went on he filled one journal and started writing in another. After several months he had a valise filled with several journals, which he studied closely almost every day.

In spite of his injured leg, Captain Fox maintained a physical training regimen that most able-bodied men would find too strenuous. Before dawn every morning he ran several miles out of the village and would return before most people were up and about. Now and then he would disappear into the nearby hills and forests with a pack slung over his back, and reappear days later disheveled and worn but obviously invigorated. Over time his presence in Songhai was no longer a curiosity to the villagers, and he became as regular a fixture in the square as the old men were.

Summer passed into autumn and then autumn into winter. When the number of travelers diminished over the winter, he spent many days in the local library reading books about the Shadow Lands, and writing copious notes into yet another set of journals. As

*winter passed and spring returned, he took his place
with the old men in the village square and watched
the variety of travelers passing through Songhai. As
before, he would introduce himself to one of the men
and converse with him over a meal or a pot of tea,
striking up acquaintances along the way. Always, Fox
wrote in his journals.*

*Another year passed and as the next spring rolled
around, Captain Fox posted several letters and
waited. As summer came, several men appeared in
Songhai one at a time. The first was a Bedouin named
Karim. Soon after came a man from the Congo. His
name was Ben Abu. Last to arrive was Jorgan, a Swiss.
Fox was pleased. Karim knew the desert, Ben Abu had
grown up in the jungle, and Jorgan had cut his teeth
on the mountains.*

*Of course, Captain Fox had come to know each of the
three men to the extent that several conversations
would allow. Apart from those conversations, he had
inquired about them and was convinced that each
brought strong credentials to his endeavor, which was
to successfully cross the Shadow Lands and map the*

region accurately. He invited the men to Songhai to explain his needs and expectations and offered them an opportunity to take part in the adventure. To a man, they accepted.

In addition to their nationalities and abilities, the three men were different in other aspects. Karim did not speak often and many times answered questions with a single word. Ben Abu was occasionally surly and picky about his food, and Jorgan found it hard to stop talking. None of them was very young, perhaps the same age as Fox himself, and each of them was thoroughly knowledgeable of the environment that he had been bred to.

The adventurers took up residence with Fox and settled into a training routine to prepare themselves for the physical demands and hardships that lay ahead. Furthermore, each of them taught the others about his specialty. Karim taught the others all he knew about the desert. Ben Abu did the same regarding the jungle, and Jorgan about the mountains. Fox outlined his plan and the route they would take on the expedition.

*A shipment arrived one day containing boxes and
bundles of tools, equipment, and weapons the men
would need to traverse the Shadow Lands. The resi-
dents of Songhai were aware of the newcomers from
far-off lands and suddenly their association with
Captain Fox came to light. Some scoffed at the foolish-
ness and audacity of anyone pitting themselves
against the unknown hardships that waited in the
Shadow Lands. The region did not bear such a name
for no reason, some said. Many predicted that Captain
Fox and his adventurers would meet the same fate as
all the others who had gone into that forbidding
region, and never returned.*

*Many of the old men in the village square listened to
such talk with a twinkle in their eyes. They had come
to know Captain Fox and he had not selected his
adventurers on a whim. "Wait and see," they advised.
"Wait and see."*

*The people of Songhai were ready to give the adven-
turers a rousing send-off, but they were surprised to
learn one day that the men had departed during the
night. For many it was a sad passing, since they never*

*expected to see Fox and his men ever again. Some
walked by his now-empty residence and sadly shook
their heads.*

*Days, weeks, and then months drifted by. No word
came of Captain Fox and his expedition. Autumn came
and then winter, but no news of the four adventurers.
The people of Songhai clucked their tongues sadly.
"Such a waste of good men," they told one another.
But as spring came with its warm days, the old men
in the village square gathered to sit in the sun and
play checkers and chess and smoke their pipes—and
occasionally glance toward the narrow road that led
toward the Shadow Lands.*

*One day after all hope of ever seeing Captain Fox and
his adventurers was long gone, four gaunt and emaci-
ated men suddenly appeared in the village square.
Their hair and beards had grown long, their clothes
torn and ragged. Evidence of injuries that had healed
was easily seen, but to a man they walked with
straight and purposeful steps. Most of their equipment had been lost or discarded and each of them
carried a pack laden with the incontrovertible proof*

of their successful adventure—samples of plants and soil, as well as precious stones. In Captain Fox's pack were journals that faithfully described every part of their journey, and maps that provided accurate details of the heretofore mysterious region.

Songhai celebrated the adventurers, who had gone into the Shadow Lands and returned to tell their tale. Music, dancing, and feasting went on for many days as every citizen of the village, young and old, shook the hand of each of the men. They noted that each of them, Captain Fox included, carried himself with an air of confidence and shared a bond, one with the other, that seemed to transcend blood and kinship. To be sure, they had forged a different kind of kinship, a kind of brotherhood, and all who perceived it were envious deep inside.

After resting and recuperating for several weeks, Karim, Ben Abu, and Jorgan went their separate ways, back to the lands and the trails they knew best. But they parted reluctantly and only after making plans for an annual reunion to commemorate and celebrate their grand adventure.

Captain Fox wrote a book that described that adventure in detail. It was hailed as the definitive work on the "conquest" of the Shadow Lands, though he and his companions did not look at it as such. The captain traveled the land and read from his book and talked about the adventure. At each town and village and coffee house he was hailed as a hero, but he was quick to tell how the skill, heart, and persistence of each of his companions had over-come obstacle after obstacle, time after time. He would tell unstintingly of how Karim had led them across the desert unerringly; about how Ben Abu's knowledge of the jungle and its ways had saved them all more than once; and how Jorgan skillfully led them over the most raw-backed, jagged, cold, and unforgiving mountains anywhere.

Many who heard his story soon realized that it was not about the taming of an unknown wilderness, or the opening up of lands heretofore unexplored. It was, instead, a story about the value of friends, good and true.

Not one warrior who knew and admired Crazy Horse had to be asked twice to join him on any excursion. But as a leader he needed to be somewhat more discerning in selecting those who followed him. The first determiner was common ground, as that was the key to survival. For example, on the evening nine days before the Battle of the Little Bighorn, Crazy Horse gathered his weapons and his horses and rode south from Ash Creek to mitigate a threat to the welfare and survival of nearly ten thousand people. Scouts had reported a column of a thousand U.S. soldiers augmented by three hundred Shoshone and Crow Indians, the latter being longtime enemies of the Lakota. This was the force commanded by Brig. Gen. George Crook on June 16, 1876, along the banks of Rosebud Creek, a few miles north of the present town of Sheridan, Wyoming.

Crazy Horse had called for fighting men to follow him to meet the enemy, knowing that there would be a significant response on two levels. The first of these was in numbers—several hundred able-bodied Lakota, Northern Cheyenne, and Northern Arapaho warriors rode out with him that evening. Second, the fighting men shared a significant common commitment. Every man was deeply dedicated to the defense of family and nation and highly motivated to do whatever was necessary to act on that commitment.

The battle began around dawn on June 17 and ended when Crazy Horse disengaged his force in mid to late afternoon. For all intents and purposes, it was a draw. Neither side could claim a decisive victory. But because Crook could neither stop Crazy Horse nor pursue and engage effectively, the Battle of the Rosebud is considered a victory for the Lakota. Crook's column from the south was one of three whose objective had been to catch the Lakota and their allies in a pincer movement. After Rosebud, Crook retreated and returned to Fort Fetterman. Crazy Horse and his men, therefore, had eliminated one-third of the pincer.

Crazy Horse depended on the skills, experience, and commitment of the men who followed him. While he probably knew every one of the other Lakota and Northern Cheyenne military leaders, logistically he could not know every fighting man personally. But he knew the kind of men they were, because they were products of the same environment in which he had trained and acquired his own values. Furthermore, everyone—warriors and leaders alike—knew that it was their duty to defend the village. It was that common denominator that gave Crazy Horse a sense of confidence.

Confidence was a critical weapon in Crazy Horse's arsenal on that pivotal day. Without it, the situation would have been tentative at best. Although we may face critical situations now and then, most of us will not be required to face a life-and-death scenario. The stakes may not literally be the injury, capture, or death of thousands of people, but our success or failure is nonetheless critical to our own circumstances. To tip the scales toward success, we can take a lesson from Crazy Horse.

Whether we think of ourselves as leaders or not, and regardless of whether we hold a leadership role in any organization, most of us must work with other people in the normal course of a job or as volunteers helping a group or organization accomplish a common purpose. Many factors must come into play in order for us to be successful in our task or mission. One of them should be a basic and necessary awareness of the people involved.

Today few of us have the advantage of growing up with the people with whom we work. Depending on our individual personalities and habits of interaction, we often identify coworkers by their jobs: Bob the planner, Jane the human resources director, and so on. Over time many of us do become better acquainted, but when five o'clock comes around we generally separate from our jobs and our coworkers as quickly as possible.

The usual thinking is, "I do what is spelled out in my job description, and so should everyone else." The assumption here is that if everyone does what is expected, then the company will achieve its mission or goals, or else the job of goal achievement belongs to somebody else. With that kind of thinking, people may as well work alone in sealed-off cubicles for eight hours a day. We must remember that there is more to life than a job or a career, and there is more to a person than the position he or she holds in an organization.

For example, at an employee picnic, a supervisor named Jack overheard a woman named Ruth, who worked in his section, mention to a coworker that she was taking skydiving lessons. His first reaction was that Ruth was something of an eccentric attention seeker. But as he listened, he heard Ruth describe her fear of heights and how skydiving was a way to conquer that fear. Jack then realized that Ruth was probably the kind of person who is not afraid to solve difficult problems and is not afraid to take risks. The next day he made it a point to note her file at work.

Weeks later, Jack was informed there would be tough negotiations with a department head over the prospect of reorganization and merging two departments, and that he should be prepared to make a case in opposition to the reorganization. He asked Ruth to write a position paper and compile supporting projections and statistics, and to help him with the negotiations. Ruth wrote a strong, concise argument and provided evidence that indicated clearly that reorganization would be counterproductive to the company. She also proved to be a steady negotiator, not afraid to face a demanding and sometimes arrogant department head. If Jack had not learned that there was more to Ruth than the basic qualifications for her job, the scenario above might not have turned out favorably. Furthermore, Jack learned even more about Ruth by simply watching her in action, and knew he could depend on her in the future to learn quickly and adapt to every situation.

Learning and adapting are critical and necessary skills, yet they are not always evident on a résumé or in a person's job title. The ability to adapt is part of character. For example, an aid organization must raise money to perform its mission to help victims of hardship. A consistent portion of their funds comes in from private contributions, but it is still necessary to conduct intensive telephone fund-raising drives at least twice a year. Since the organization has a small administrative staff, it relies on a volunteer base to carry out its objectives, including fund-raising.

For the telephone campaign, the staff has a small group of volunteers who are always available, but they must also train new people. For the campaign to be effective, the telephone solicitation—which is cold calling—has to be concise and professional, but not to the extent that it would be considered "slick." The staff has learned that no one can be trained to be a telephone solicitor in ten easy lessons; people either have the aptitude for it, or not. So the organization reviews the backgrounds of its volunteer base and selects those who have the appropriate experience.

The commitment of the volunteers is not the primary concern in this instance. Volunteers sign on because they believe in and support the basic mission and purpose of the organization. For the telephone campaign, the organization needs a specific skill and prior experience in the area of sales, and in this case it is critical for the organization to "know its friends." Salespeople regularly do the kind of cold calling that is needed in this instance. By putting them on the phones, the organization increases its chances for a successful fund-raiser. In other words, the skills and abilities are appropriate to the task.

Once funds are raised, they can be allocated to the basic mission of the organization, which is to help families in times of hardship. This assistance is provided primarily by volunteers, and it follows that the primary requirement to be a volunteer is willingness to serve. After volunteers are accepted, they can be trained according to the organization's structure and specific methods of operation. But since it exists to help people in times of duress, volunteers must be sensitive not only to the tangible needs of the people it helps—such as food, shelter, or clothing—but be just as sensitive to their state of mind. People can be taught to distribute blankets or food, but basic values such as compassion and empathy are part of a person's character. Once again, the organization matches the habits, character, or values of its volunteers to the task.

During the pre-reservation period, one of the most critical roles for Lakota warriors was that of a scout. Scouts were the eyes and ears of military leaders and, to perform that necessary mission, they had to be highly skilled, rugged, virtually fearless, self-confident, and, capable of surviving alone in the wild in every season of the year. Mature warriors learned to be scouts under the careful guidance and tutelage of those more experienced in the role. No military leader would ask anyone who was not adequately qualified to undertake such a risky task. Scouts were the elite among warriors, and Lakota scouts were entitled to use a distinctive symbol—three yellow horizontal lines—on their personal accoutrements to signify their status. Many scouts were also members of the Crazy Dog or Kit Fox warrior societies.

Crazy Horse trusted the ability of his fellow scouts, and those whose character he knew he trusted implicitly. He would not hesitate to accept the information they provided at face value or to ask a scout to take on a risky or dangerous mission alone or lead other warriors in battle. On the evening of the aforementioned Battle of the Rosebud, it was a scout (or perhaps two) who brought Crazy Horse a report on the advance of Brig. Gen. George Crook's force north along the Shining Mountains, toward the Little Bighorn. He may have asked questions to get a clearer understanding, but he did not question the validity of the report itself.

The day after the Little Bighorn, an intense debate raged over what to do about the Reno–Benteen detachment, surrounded and besieged above the Little Bighorn River. Scouts arrived from the north with reports of more soldiers—two columns, as a matter of fact, one under the command of Maj. Gen. Alfred Terry and the other led by Col. John Gibbon. The two columns combined were a force of 1,500. Again, Crazy Horse did not question the veracity of the report and agreed with the decision to move the encampment out of harm's way. He and the other battle leaders knew that such a large force had much more firepower than the Lakota and Northern Cheyenne could put into the field, especially given the fact that they had just fought three engagements in two days and expended much of their ammunition. Because Crazy Horse and other military leaders trusted the ability of those scouts and had no doubt as to the accuracy of their information, they had no issue with the decision to take their women, children, and elderly south toward the Bighorn Mountains.

Though Crazy Horse was well known throughout the Lakota, Dakota, and Nakota nation, most people knew him only by his reputation and through the stories they heard from those who had actually seen or followed him. Many of the people who came to the gathering that culminated in the Battle of the Little Bighorn had never seen Crazy Horse before, much less fought alongside him. Yet they knew his character well enough to follow his lead.

It is likely, however, that only a few people knew Crazy Horse intimately: his parents, an uncle or two, his brother and sister, his wife, and his friends He Dog, Lone Bear, Hump, Touch the Clouds, Stands in Timber, Chips, and Spotted Tail. Those people knew him as a person, without the mantle and responsibility of leadership. They saw him being thoughtful, angry, puzzled, grieving, joyful, determined, and tender. They saw him laugh and cry over the trials and tribulations of everyday life, and agonize about the future. They heard him express frustration, doubt, optimism, pride, and many other human emotions. Likewise, he knew them and shared with them the good and bad moments of life.

For different reasons and in different ways, a bond of trust was established between Crazy Horse and his intimate companions and fellow fighting men. When people know they can depend on one another, they are powerful. This is the kind of power upon which cooperation, allegiance, alliance, devotion, and dedication are formed. When people share this kind of trust and empowerment, then no problem, task, or objective seems impossible—be it a buffalo hunt, a battle, erecting a lodge, or the prospect of facing a grim future.

If Crazy Horse's relatives, friends, and followers had not trusted him, they would not have followed him to Fort Robinson to give control to a group of people they all detested. They all trusted that he would do what was best for them. Likewise, he trusted that everyone would be strong in the face of the unknown difficulties that lay ahead.

Under those extremely trying circumstances, the best way to face the unknown was to rely on what they knew of one another. This is no less true for us as individuals, communities, societies, and nations today. Fortunately there are less tragic examples for us to consider. One is the alliance between the Lakota, Northern Cheyenne, and Northern Arapaho people. That relationship flourished for many generations, to the point where all three groups spoke one another's language. Consequently, many people among them were trilingual.

Each of the tribes had their own entanglements with white people and the U.S. government—most tragically for the Cheyenne and the Arapaho at Sand Creek, Colorado, and the Washita River, Oklahoma. After Sand Creek, the Arapaho and Cheyenne called on relatives and friends among the Lakota to launch revenge raids. The greatest victory shared by that alliance was at the Little Bighorn in June 1876. Through extremely difficult times, the alliance never wavered. To this day, the three nations remain friends.

This kind of mutual empowerment did not die out with the pre-reservation era. Jack and Ruth, from the earlier contemporary example, had it. Soldiers have it when they depend on one another in combat. A high school or college sports team that plays together as a unit, as opposed to a collection of highly skilled athletes playing for individual records, has that power.

A ready-made friend or ally can be someone who faces the same struggles or is trying to accomplish the same things we are, someone who shares the same values we do, or someone whose character matches our own. Knowing our friends means identifying with their situations and struggles, and buying into their goals. Keeping our friends also means interacting unselfishly with them by showing them that we share their victories and setbacks. In essence, what happens to one part of the friendship equation happens to all parts of it.

Alliances and friendships are not forged for sharing the good times. We form them to help one another through the difficult times and the most trying situations. When we stand by our friends through their hard times, we show them that they can trust us; and that ensures that they will be there for us when we need them. No leader—no matter how motivated, dedicated, or qualified—can do it alone.

THE THIRD PRINCIPLE: KNOW YOUR ENEMIES

Whether we like it or not, the fact of the matter is that we live in a world where we face constant threats individually and as a collective. Adversity has always been part of our existence. No matter how weak or strong we are, the world has always been a dangerous place. Difficulty, discomfort, adversity, and danger are burdens—to the extent that anything that threatens to change our well-being, our happiness, or our status quo for the worse is regarded as "enemy."

On the national level, anything or anyone that threatens our security is the enemy. Here in this country we are told regularly that the world is against us and that we should always be vigilant and afraid. We even have a color code in a graduated scale to determine the appropriate fear level for the day, from concern all the way to panic! Then there may be anxiety and fear if we don't know the color code for the day: We might spend a day not being afraid enough, or too afraid. If that isn't enough to worry about, then we have consider that not being afraid enough—or not being afraid at all or being unaware of the color codes of fear—might be regarded as unpatriotic, which could bring its own consequences. And then, when we realize that the entire process is designed to control us, we become afraid that someone will realize that we have figured out the program. Clearly, our civilization has evolved to the point that worry and fear are everyday aspects of our lives. The example itself is no less realistic for its absurdity, and reflects the very palpable "us against them" stance to which we have become conditioned.

No one in his or her right mind wants an enemy. But enemies and adversarial relationships are a fact of life for every kind of living thing, and have been for longer than we care to know. Before Europeans happened onto North America, many of the indigenous peoples chose a philosophical view of enemies that was based on practical reality. Many would say that the worth of a nation was measured by the power of its enemies. This may be the basis for the saying that whatever doesn't kill you will make you stronger. While people probably would have preferred not to have enemies, they nonetheless accepted that they were part of real life. That reality brought about a choice: People either stood up to their enemies or succumbed. To stand up to them consistently, a nation or tribe had to be strong. Therefore, an enemy taught you the necessity for strength and watchfulness.

The Lakota of old knew their enemies: To the northwest were the Crow people in present-day Montana, east of the mountains and along the Yellowstone River. North along the Missouri River, and to the south and west of it, were the Arikara, eventual allies with the Mandan and Hidatsa, in present-day south-central North Dakota. The Omaha were southeast of Lakota territory, along the banks of the Missouri in present-day Nebraska. The Pawnee were to the south in what is now southern Nebraska and northern Kansas. Far to the west were the Eastern Shoshone, in what is now west-central Wyoming.

Among all of the Lakota and their traditional enemies, the folklore is replete with stories of battles and excursions into one another's territories. There were frequent clashes and pitched battles, and much blood was spilled. Hatred and ethnocentrism often ran high. Nevertheless, the Lakota respected their enemies. That respect came from in-depth knowledge.

In the interest of basic survival it was necessary to know as much as possible about anything and anyone that was a threat to life, home, and territory. Scouts were constantly sent into enemy territory to observe and report. Consequently, the tribes on the northern plains knew one another well despite being separated by vast distances and different languages. They knew one another's cultural values, hunting patterns, military strengths and weaknesses, and whether they were friend or foe—information specific to the point of knowing who the head man was among various groups and bands within the neighboring tribes.

Knowing the enemy was an integral part of defending against them. In the process of watching the borders for any enemy, they discovered just who was crossing them. This revealed several factors about the enemy, not the least of which were weaponry, tactical ability and tendencies, fighting ability, and so on. Lakota warriors would meet the enemy, whether known or unknown, and significantly improved their chances for victory.

As part of their warrior training, every generation of Lakota fighting men was taught about their enemies. They learned that, in most cases, animosities were generations and hundreds of years old. But the information, stories, and folklore were also shared with the entire community. Every adult in the village knew who the enemies were.

Civilian and military leaders counted on up-to-date information, but they were unable to personally gather information all of the time. They relied on an elite group of men as their eyes and ears: the scouts. Though all Lakota males were capable of surviving in the wilderness in any season of the year, not all of them had the mind-set to spend days and weeks alone in enemy territory.

That required a highly motivated, dedicated, and extremely self-confident individual skilled in the art of stealth and camouflage, one capable of enduring a variety of physical hardships in order to carry out his responsibility. And because enough of them did, the leaders were usually aware of the enemies around them.

Despite their difficult and sometimes bloody histories, a kind of relationship existed between those traditional native enemies who knew and understood one another so well. This relationship was based in mutual respect. Interestingly, animosities were sometimes put aside on the simple basis of ancient enemies giving their word that there would be no hostilities. One well-known instance occurred in 1851, when several tribes gathered at Fort Laramie in what is now southeastern Wyoming.

Ironically, the gathering took place at the largely selfish request of a newcomer to the northern plains: Euro-Americans. By that point, the whites were already showing every indication that they would become a formidable enemy. In all, the Blackfeet; the Mandan, Hidatsa, and Arikara (now known as the Three Affiliated Tribes of North Dakota); Crow; Cheyenne; and Arapaho all came to Fort Laramie, along with the Lakota, Dakota, and Nakota (the alliance known to the whites as the Sioux). Most of the tribes had come based on the promise of gifts from the Euro-Americans—which were significantly late in arriving—as well as for the opportunity to compile substantive information about this new adversary.

The Blackfeet, who were then and are still in what is now northwest Montana, were comparable in population to the Lakota, Dakota, and Nakota nation, had clashed with most or all of the other tribes at one time or another. The animosity between the Crow and the Lakota was hundreds of years old, and therefore the Crow were enemies to the Cheyenne and Arapaho since those two tribes were Lakota allies. Caught in the mix were the Mandan, Hidatsa, and Arikara who, only because they were significantly smaller in population, tried to avoid conflicts with the Lakota. Individually, of course, fighting men from any of these tribes were not necessarily afraid of one another one-on-one, but the more populous tribes—such as the Blackfeet and Lakota—had a definite numerical advantage if it came down to all-out warfare. That was a reality not ignored by the smaller tribes. Therefore, when all of these tribes came together at Fort Laramie in the summer of 1851 (often referred to as the Council at Long Meadows), there was certainly an atmosphere of hostility. This was partially because of the whites, who were an unknown factor, but mostly because of the history of clashes and warfare between the various tribes.

Hostilities can be set aside, but feelings and attitudes cannot. Yet in spite of that, each side knew that the other would honor the truce because they had given their word. Feelings and attitudes aside, the tribes knew one another well enough to know there existed a sense of honor, and that this cultural value that they all shared would be more than enough to prevent hostilities. Of course, the Euro-Americans came away from the Fort Laramie experience with a sense that they had been in control of the situation and had earned the respect and fear of the tribes. They were wrong on both counts.

The interaction between the various tribes on the northern plains was many generations old. Although by the middle of the 1800s there was certainly an awareness that the Euro-Americans represented a new threat, none of the tribes had reliable information about the people themselves. At best their interactions and encounters had been brief, and because the first white people on the scene came singly or in small groups, there was no inkling among any of the western tribes as to their actual numbers. The combined population of the approximately sixty tribes on the Great Plains was probably 300,000. Therefore, the various tribes on the northern plains assessed, by obvious indicators such as appearance and physical stature, clothing, weapons, tools, and lifestyle, that they still held the upper hand. What they could not have known at the time was that the population of white people in the east was already more than 20 million.

Soon enough, however, the Lakota had the opportunity to add to their knowledge of Euro-Americans as they watched the migration of white emigrants along the Oregon Trail, a two-thousand-mile road from Missouri to Oregon. Every summer for twenty years, hundreds of wagons filled with thousands of people crossed through Lakota lands. In the beginning, just as the Council at Long Meadows had been, the Oregon Trail experience was a curiosity for the Lakota. The first instances of face-to-face contact between emigrants and Lakota were nonconfrontational, albeit tense and suspicious on both sides. Yet, unaware that the emigrants were leaving bad circumstances in hopes of finding a better life somewhere else, the Lakota saw only the obvious movement of wagons, livestock, and thousands and thousands of people and knew that it could only turn out to be a problem.

Still, although soldiers were posted in the forts along and within Lakota territory, they did not impress the Lakota with their military prowess. The most impressive things about them were their firearms. It was not until several years later, when Lakota leaders began travel to Washington, D.C., that they confirmed earlier suspicions that the power of the Euro-Americans also lay in their numbers. Indeed, by the time of the migration, 350,000 Euro-Americans had made the trek on the Oregon Trail.

In 1855 the Lakota experienced the first major military clash with white soldiers. Gen. William S. Harney out of Fort Kearny (in central Nebraska) launched a punitive campaign to punish the Lakota, who had retaliated to an attack by Lieut. John Grattan and wiped out thirty men, including Grattan himself. Harney's two-thousand-man force found and surrounded a Sicangu Lakota camp along the Blue Water Creek in what is now north-central Nebraska. The Lakota came out on the short end of a brief and violent clash, in which several of their head men—Spotted Tail, Little Thunder, and Iron Shell—were severely wounded after a surprise attack. The most tragic consequence of the Battle of Blue Water was the killing, mutilation, and capture of nearly a hundred women and children. This was the beginning of a serious change in Lakota attitude toward whites.

After that attack, the young Crazy Horse (then still called Light Hair) came back to a burned-out village along the Blue Water to find dead and mutilated bodies. This gut-wrenching experience would remain the basis for his attitude and actions toward white people from that point forward.

It is worth noting that the reaction to the Euro-American enemy varied among the major Lakota leaders. Spotted Tail of the Sicangu Lakota, for example, realized early on that the strength of the whites was in their numbers. A brief imprisonment at

Fort Leavenworth, Kansas, gave him a firsthand glimpse into Euro-American power. So, in the late 1860s, this physically powerful warrior decided that survival among the whites was the best alternative for his people and agreed to his own agency near Camp Robinson, in northwest Nebraska. In 1868 Red Cloud, an Oglala Lakota, also agreed to his own agency near Fort Robinson for basically the same reasons as Spotted Tail. Other leaders such as Swift Bear of the Sicangu and Touch the Clouds of the Mniconju also tacitly agreed that continued hostilities with the whites would mean innocent women and children being killed, not to mention total loss of land.

For Sitting Bull and Crazy Horse the basic issue of trust was the primary factor for their continued resistance. They knew that the whites would not keep their word. Sitting Bull, in fact, sent messages to other Lakota leaders urging them not to negotiate with the whites over land or sign any paper offered by them. For these two leaders, living under the control of white people was not a sensible option. Their opinions and decisions were based primarily on what they knew of the character of white people, or the lack thereof. They were not unaware of the military advantages the whites held, but they probably felt that those factors could be mitigated by better fighting men using better tactics.

By the mid-1870s, however, Crazy Horse realized that, in addition to taking land, the basic objective of the white soldiers was to kill as many Lakota as possible. Historians like to say that he emulated the superior field tactics of the U.S. Army, but in reality it was the Lakota who had the superior tactics and better-trained fighting men. Crazy Horse tried to convince other Lakota military leaders that their most effective tactic against the soldiers would be to kill as many of them as possible. Because their enemy did not fight by the Lakota codes of honor and respect, he knew that the Lakota would have to fight a war of attrition, just like the Euro-American invaders, if there was to be any chance of driving them out of Lakota territory.

Still, in comparison to the knowledge the Lakota had regarding their native enemies, their understanding of Euro-Americans was woefully inadequate. For example, they had no way of knowing about Gen. William Tecumseh Sherman's total war strategy, used effectively against the South in the Civil War, wherein he laid waste to the enemy's environment and, thereby, destroyed the resources that the people and the army of the South needed to live and continue to wage war. Had the Lakota known this, or the fact that General Sherman was the chief advisor to President Ulysses S. Grant on matters concerning native people, their reaction to him would have been different. It was, after all, General Sherman who invited "sportsmen" to hunt bison (buffalo) on the plains, knowing the decimation of the great herds was the most effective way to defeat the Lakota.

Ironically, the Lakota epitomized both the benefits and the dangerous necessity of knowing the enemy. On the one hand, they thoroughly knew their ancient native enemies, largely because of generations of interaction with them. On the other hand, although it was evident early on that the whites were aggressive, the Lakota made the grave mistake of not recognizing the true nature and intent of the Euro-Americans: that they were imperialistic and came with the intent to colonize and control.

Had the Lakota known more about the enemy from the east, perhaps their military strategy and tactics would have been different, and perhaps they would have taken a different approach at the negotiating table. But even if the Lakota had been successful in altering the way things happened, the eventual outcome of the so-called clash of cultures would only have been prolonged. In the end, the overwhelming number of Euro-Americans was the one factor that exponentially strengthened their other advantages, such as technology, imperialism, and ethnocentrism.

In the end, the Lakota respected the military and numerical strength of this enemy that changed their world. The so-called Indian Wars have long been over, at least militarily (except for the 1973 standoff at Wounded

Knee, South Dakota). Yet the adversarial relationship between the Lakota and the U.S. government still goes on. The present-day Lakota know their enemies, although they are now called "obstacles" or "challenges": among them are apathy, ethnocentrism, and racism. The battlegrounds have changed to courtrooms, but the people have no choice but to continue fighting for the same reason Crazy Horse, Sitting Bull, Spotted Tail, Red Cloud, and other leaders did: survival. It remains to be seen what will happen culturally and legally, especially where issues such as tribal sovereignty are concerned. Past victories and, especially, past losses will always serve as valuable lessons to *know the enemy*.

Regardless of whether we choose to adopt a philosophical outlook toward our enemies, let us not make the mistake of thinking they do not exist. Whether they assault us unfairly or we have created them by our own ignorance or arrogance, they are out there. But to realistically understand their intentions and capabilities, we need to grow up and look beyond the labels we tend to apply to them.

An astute and honest leader will endeavor to understand our enemies and their reasons for disliking, despising, and fearing us. Furthermore, a good leader will be honest with the public, rather than fanning the flames of fear with labels, characterizations, excuses, or outright lies.

It is interesting to note that the oath taken by most government officials contains a line that speaks to defending against "enemies foreign and domestic." That statement is either a realistic assumption that enemies opposed to our ideologies can and do exist among us, or it is nothing more than a blanket expression of paranoia. If it is the latter, we must remember that paranoia is never the basis for logical and critical thinking. It has been and always will be the basis for knee-jerk reaction. Dangerous and persistent enemies are indeed justifications for strength and vigilance, but they should not be reasons to let paranoia run rampant. Paranoia leads to suspicion and misguided fear of anything and anyone, which leads to a *kill them all and let God sort them out* mentality. To assume that God is on the side of that kind of an attitude is the epitome of arrogance.

It might seem that enemies also exist in our personal or professional lives. Inflation, bad weather, business competition, layoffs, and chronic illness, for example, are certainly not to be ignored. Such realities must be faced and mitigated in order to ensure normality, happiness, and success. Yet as bothersome and tough as they can be to overcome, they are not enemies—not in comparison to poverty, homelessness, loneliness, racism, indifference, ethnocentrism, disease, disaster, ignorance, arrogance, and apathy. These enemies can defeat us from within and cause the downfall of any society, much like an enemy that may lay siege from the outside.

Strength is obviously a deterrent against outside aggression or outright attack. A strong military prepared to go to the wall to defend the homeland is necessary, given that humankind has proven time and time again that the penchant for aggression, covetousness, imperialism, greed, egomania, and ethnocentrism will never diminish. But while we expend a great portion of our economic resources guarding our seas, borders, and skies against enemies from the outside, one wonders whether we shouldn't be paying as much if not more attention to the enemies within.

If we know our enemies, we tend to focus on their military assets in terms of manpower, level of training, weaponry, and usual tactics. We also know of their past performance in military conflicts and the ideology that drives them. We determine what kind of assets we will need to expend to suppress them, as well as the level of material and personnel losses we might experience. In the same manner we should know what it would take to mitigate and even defeat poverty and homelessness. We should know what kind of efforts and resources must be brought to bear to eliminate racism and ethnocentrism, and what it would take to reduce the effect of disease and mitigate the effects of disaster, for example. We need to know this because these are the kinds of enemies that attack the spirit and soul of any society.

That these kinds of enemies exist among and within us is readily evident. One needs only to turn on any television news program to see the face of ethnocentrism and apathy and to hear their voices. Ethnocentrism and bigotry speak through celebrities, public officials, or members of the media who use invectives—against any group—with a sense of entitlement and impunity. Apathy is apparently alive and well when, two years after a devastating hurricane, the federal government's most powerful relief agency is still more concerned about its own rules and policies than about providing relief and hope to victims who are still suffering.

The spirit and soul of any society, of any nation, should be more important than economic and military strength. When all segments of society understand the causes of poverty, bigotry, ignorance, apathy, and homelessness and work to eliminate them, there is character. Such character enhances and tempers any other kind of strength. Therefore, the sign of a strong society should not be the number of its weapons or the size of its military, but how quickly, efficiently, and compassionately it takes care of its less fortunate citizens. As discussed in the previous chapter, a strong society leads to a strong warrior class.

Apathy, arrogance, and greed cannot be profiled in the same way that we try to conveniently categorize an enemy that professes to a different ideology or takes up a gun against us. To those internal enemies we cannot ascribe race, color, or creed, because they can take hold in any mind and any heart. Those are the enemies of every society, every culture, and every nation. Therefore, those societies, cultures, or nations that recognize the power and persistence of such enemies are those that will remain strong.

To engage and defeat poverty, homelessness, bigotry, apathy, ignorance, and arrogance we must understand their nature, which is to weaken and erode a little at a time, in such a manner that we do not realize what is happening until it is too late. Suddenly there is an epidemic of arrogance because we have forgotten what respect for others is. Suddenly our awareness and the edges of our towns and cities are littered with homeless people because we have lost the ability to be compassionate. Many of those homeless are veterans of war, and that tragic reality begs the question: How strong is a nation that essentially ignores its own warriors? What does the reality of hundreds of thousands of homeless veterans say about the moral strength of the country they served?

The sad reality is that a nation with the economic might to put men on the moon and send million-dollar missiles whistling toward an enemy in a millisecond cannot find the collective heart to help its most needful citizens. Perhaps the overabundance of technology, military might, and self-obsession has left us little room for compassion. Perhaps apathy and indifference are too great as enemies. Or perhaps not?

One powerful antidote to ethnocentrism is demonstrated when parents, teachers, community leaders, and elected officials denounce it publicly and show that while it may be fodder for media with a ratings-driven penchant for sensational news, it is not the predominant attitude of the community, the society, or the nation. Similarly, while the federal government may be slow to respond and help victims of disasters, other relief agencies step in to get the job done in spite of the fact they have only a fraction of the resources and manpower in comparison. They also aptly demonstrate that a sense of purpose fueled by compassion is an effective deterrent to apathy and ineptitude.

Poverty, apathy, ignorance, racism, and other social ills are obviously not conventional enemies in the sense that they do not field armies, launch invasions, or stockpile weapons of mass destruction. They are, however, as persistent, insidious, and deadly as any enemy, conventional or otherwise. Furthermore, they cannot be faced and confronted by armies fighting on foreign soil. These enemies must be faced by every ordinary person, in the course of daily life, because that is the battleground. Among those who lead the fight are parents, civic and religious leaders, and teachers. But in front of them should be county commissioners, mayors, governors, and presidents doing more than the expected posturing and uttering more than the expected rhetoric. Their responsibility is to eliminate these particular enemies and mitigate the problems they cause.

The survival of individuals, societies, and nations is dependent on vigilance and the willingness to stand up against enemies that threaten. But to survive and thrive, we must know our enemies for what they are. We must remind ourselves that it is easier to see enemies that exist in the physical world, and much more difficult to see those that may dwell within us all. Many times the enemies that are more difficult to understand are harder to defeat. But we need only to observe what happens in our daily lives to perceive their presence.

In the 1970s a large public school district on the northern plains with a significant native enrollment saw that many children had consecutive absences. Of course, extended absences had a negative impact on the absent child's performance in the classroom. Many of them fell behind in their work and had to struggle to catch up, and many were unable to do so.

In checking attendance records of all native students from kindergarten through high school, the district superintendent discovered that extended absences were overwhelmingly more frequent among native students than non-native students. To circumvent the problem, he recommended to the school board that strong penalties be established and enforced. He was certain that the prospect of staying after school, losing the privilege of participating in athletics, or being expelled would motivate the native students to come to school.

On the day the school board was considering the superintendent's recommendations, a group of native parents attended the meeting and stated their opposition. They explained to the school board that many of the extended absences of native children occurred when there was a death in the immediate or extended family. It was a custom for native families to observe certain rituals that occurred over a period of days, and these longstanding traditions had been in place for many generations before the establishment of reservations and schools.

The debate among the school board members was contentious. Though some of them understood that their ignorance of local native tradition was part of the problem, most of them insisted that school board policies were more important to the social welfare of native children than old traditions. Consequently, they voted to implement the superintendent's recommendations. It would not be until after that superintendent had retired that the issue was once again debated, and the school board relaxed its policy somewhat.

Though the importance of education is a popular subject of campaign rhetoric every other year, it is still not supported consistently by governmental resources. Rural and inner-city schools consistently face limited—and in many instances severely limited— funding. Lack of adequate funding affects a school system in every area, especially teacher salaries and textbooks. Though just about every politician, especially at the national level, denounces the travesty and promises to study the situation to find a solution, they then vote for military spending to the tune of billions of dollars without batting an eye. American students are scoring lower in mathematics and sciences in comparison to students from many other countries. It's apparently an acceptable trade-off as long as we remain the number-one military power on the face of the earth. Being the proverbial biggest kid on the global block is apparently more important than basic education.

Consider a teenager who earns a high-school diploma from a school forced to find creative ways to raise money for textbooks and barely adequate pay for its teachers. In an ironic twist, that high-school graduate joins the navy and becomes a weapons technician;

and it is his finger on the button that fires a million-dollar missile, which flies for less than a minute to its target. Rough math shows an expenditure rate of nearly seventeen thousand dollars per second, on its way to causing death and destruction. We can well imagine what that cash-strapped school system would have been able to do with that same amount of money. Practically and philosophically, it would have served life rather than cause death.

Ordinary people have two basic choices in the face of indifference and the other enemies that plague us: We can do nothing or we can do something. Either choice has consequences, of course. Doing nothing empowers apathy, indifference, racism, and so on. It certainly empowers those civic, religious, and political leaders whose priority is other than the well-being of their constituency.

Leaders are only a small part of any society, but what they say and do commands widespread attention. In comparison, the everyday actions of ordinary individuals receive little or no attention. Nevertheless, it is these ordinary people who influence family and community more than most leaders can. When a couple distributes food and blankets to homeless people, their unheralded act of compassion is far and away more powerful than the indifferent platitudes on the "homeless problem" uttered by politicians. And when ordinary people take it upon themselves to hold their leaders accountable for their actions and inactions, then there is potential for more widespread change. Those who know and understand their enemies, and are willing to do what it takes to defeat them, can rightfully expect their leaders to do the same.

THE FOURTH PRINCIPLE: TAKE THE LEAD

If we abide by the definition of a leader as one who influences the actions and attitudes of others, the next logical question is: *How?* The only obvious answer is by example.

To know yourself honestly, to know your friends or those who struggle, work, or fight alongside you, and to know the enemy are all hallmarks of the intellect of any leader. Knowledge and experience rest in the mind of a leader, therefore, but character rises out of the heart. And it is only from the heart that one can lead by example.

There were many renowned leaders among the Lakota: Spotted Tail and Swift Bear of the Sicangu (also known as Brulé); Lone Horn, Touch the Clouds, and Big Foot of the Mniconju; Sitting Bull and Gall of the Hunkpapa; and Man Whose Enemies Are Afraid of His

Horses, Bull Bear, Good Road, and Crazy Horse of the Oglala. These are but a few. Those who preceded them set the standards they followed. Each one of those men knew, however, that there was only one way to lead: by taking the lead or setting the example.

In September 1855, when Gen. William Harney arrived at Little Thunder's village on Blue Water Creek and demanded a parley with the Sicangu, three leaders rose to the occasion: Spotted Tail, Little Thunder, and Iron Shell. The soldiers had appeared so unexpectedly that Spotted Tail and the other men, it is said, hurried unarmed to meet Harney before he reached the village. They sat down with the general and several of his officers, and Harney brashly demanded that the men who killed Lieutenant Grattan the year before be turned over to him. Unbeknownst to the Sicangu, while Harney was haranguing, the rest of his soldiers were surrounding the village about a mile away. When they attacked, Spotted Tail and the other leaders realized that they had fallen for a ruse and immediately stood to fight.

Almost at once, Spotted Tail was stabbed in the shoulder with a sword, the blade slicing completely through and protruding from his back. At well over six feet tall, Spotted Tail demonstrated more than just physical strength. He pulled the sword out of his shoulder and killed a soldier with it—likely the one who had stabbed him—and then fought tenaciously.

Before he was wounded grievously a second time, he managed to kill or wound several other soldiers. By all accounts, Little Thunder and Iron Shell held their own, as well.

The Battle of the Blue Water was a tragic loss for the Sicangu. Women and children were killed and captured, Spotted Tail's daughter among the captives. But from that encounter came stories of the courage of Spotted Tail, Little Thunder, and Iron Shell under fire and their actions during the hand-to-hand fighting. They were nothing less than heroic and became examples for boys and fledgling warriors to emulate.

Spotted Tail recovered from his wounds and was eventually reunited with his family. Harney eventually marched north after a brief stop at Fort Laramie, threatening death and mayhem as he went, dubbed by the Sicangu as Woman Killer. A year or two later, Spotted Tail demonstrated his courage yet again, this time letting himself be imprisoned for an alleged crime he did not commit—and which, for that matter, was not committed by any Lakota. But he knew the whites would not be dissuaded from punishing some Lakota, so he offered himself up. Honoring songs were sung as he was hauled away to Fort Leavenworth because the Sicangu believed they would never see their leader alive again. But, not surprisingly, he did survive the ordeal and returned to the northern plains, where he assumed his position as head man of the Sicangu. Once again his undaunted courage became the basis for a hero story.

As a young man, Crazy Horse had heard many hero stories and knew that leadership was a daunting responsibility. Although he aspired to be a warrior, as all Lakota boys did, he did not necessarily want to be a leader. Yet because he set himself apart by his conspicuous actions as a fighting man, other warriors naturally looked to him.

After the Battle of the Hundred in the Hand, the American detachment in Fort Phil Kearny was understandably leery of venturing outside the walls of the fort. The winter that year was extremely harsh and the Lakota, Northern Cheyenne, and Arapaho villages up and down the Tongue River valley were as affected by the conditions as the Americans inside the fort. Food supplies ran low and hunters had to pursue game in deep snow and bitterly cold weather. Crazy Horse and his younger brother, Little Hawk, then in his late teens, were among many who risked their lives to hunt for fresh meat. On one occasion they were away from the safety of their village and warmth of their parents' lodge for several days, trekking through the snow on snowshoes.

For Crazy Horse, it was not a question of whether or not he should go out hunting. A year earlier, in the summer of 1865, he had been given the honor of being selected as a Shirt Wearer, or Shirt Man. The making of Shirt Wearers was an ancient tradition, and a distinction given to men of high character. The honor was named for the elaborately decorated shirts that these men were given, made from the tanned hides of bighorn sheep. Included in the decorations were strands of human hair. Each strand represented a combat honor, yet the hair was not taken from scalped enemies (they were donated by female family members). It was said that young Crazy Horse's shirt had about a hundred strands.

The status was largely ceremonial, as no Shirt Wearer had the authority or leeway to tell anyone else how to live their lives. Rather, they were expected to influence others through their own high standards—their words and deeds. Though ceremonial, the position held power, because recipients were selected by the people and expected to lead by example through experience, character, and commitment. Interestingly, however, because of the changes occurring in Oglala Lakota society at the time, Crazy Horse and his three fellow Oglala Shirt Wearers—American Horse, Young Man Afraid of His Horse, and Sword—were the last to ever be given that distinction.

The times in which Crazy Horse lived encompassed many dramatic events that continue to fascinate, even today. For most people, however, that interest seems to wane for the period after 1890. The assumption is that nothing dramatic or important happened after the massacre at Wounded Knee. Yet it was during the period from 1877 to 1940 when the Lakota people faced their severest tests, because they had to adapt to a totally different lifestyle under duress. During that period the federal government concentrated their efforts on giving the Lakota an "extreme makeover," attempting to change the entire culture. Government and parochial boarding schools used radical measures to strip them of language and lifeways. And just in case boarding schools did not succeed, Congress passed legislation to solidify the government's course of forced assimilation.

One of the acts passed by Congress was the Indian Reorganization Act (IRA) of 1934. Among other things, the IRA set forth a mechanism for self-government among the Indian tribes—implying in one way or another that such a concept was something new to them. But of course, it was not. For the Lakota, as with other tribes, a council of elders had served more or less as an informal type of government, to put it in terms that non-native people can understand. A council functioned by and large in every village or community and the only requirement for membership was to have lived long enough to earn the distinction of elder. Such experience and knowledge was the basis for wisdom, and it was wisdom that was the strength of the village council.

The IRA model, on the other hand, gave Indian tribes the "right" to fashion their governments as an elected tribal council—a council chairman or president elected by the council—and a court system. Essentially, this established a legislative, executive, and judicial branch. Later, tribal chairmen and presidents were elected at large by popular vote.

One requirement for membership to the IRA councils undermined the pre-reservation, pre-IRA cultural concept of the council: The minimum age to stand for election was usually twenty-five. There was some doubt and discontent among many Lakota communities in reaction to that requirement, because young men simply did not have the experience or knowledge to lead in this way. Because the Lakota people still realized the necessity for experience and knowledge, the first elected tribal councils were for the most part comprised of older men. Of course, the early tribal councilmen knew that eventually younger and younger men would be elected to the councils. Still, they did what they could to advise their constituents that the IRA council was really the only game in town, and that it was better to do what they could to make it their own. By serving as councilmen in a system that, to them, was inherently flawed, those first tribal council members essentially set the example for the generations that would follow them. They tried to show that it was better to have some form of self-government than none at all.

During those years of the early reservation period, good leadership from within was the one thing the Lakota needed as they adjusted to living in a way that was totally foreign to them. The people still remembered the old ways, and they still knew and understood the principles of the Shirt Wearers. That first generation of tribal council members led the way by showing that the Lakota had to make the best of an undesirable situation for the sake of survival. The example, and indeed the spirit, of Crazy Horse, Spotted Tail, Sitting Bull, and others lived on during those unspectacular but difficult years.

Those men who served on the first IRA councils on the Lakota reservations in the 1930s and 1940s knew that they were the focal points of transition from the old ways to the new. And they knew that what they did would carry more weight than what they said. Therein is a critical lesson for anyone in any type of leadership role or position.

Even a society in which citizens have the right to pick and choose, their leaders cannot ensure that good or even adequate leaders will come forward to be chosen. Although the very nature of the system will guarantee that there will always be a wide array of candidates, there is one significant downside: Most or all of the candidates who stand for election, especially to high-level state and national offices, are *politicians*. This is a downside because politicians will never forget who put them in office— those large contributors that enabled a successful campaign. Second, their first and predominant allegiance is to the party line, and only after that to the citizenry at large. Rare is the politician who is truly impartial, honoring the duties and responsibilities of his or her office without favoritism. This unfortunate reality is further exacerbated by the existence of political parties.

The long history of political parties implies that they really are necessary, one of the justifications for which being the assertion that they foster diverse viewpoints and ideology. Despite that worn-out argument, a diversity of viewpoints and political ideologies exist and does arise without their influence.

In reality, politicians need the affiliation of a political party to have validity as a candidate in the perception of the voting public. Political parties exist to espouse and sell their ideologies, first and foremost. Though they may seem to care about the welfare of the people, self-perpetuation is the first priority. They care little for the people's opinion on issues of national concern, such as poverty, homelessness, affordable health care, racism, foreign policy, or questionable leadership. Though politicians and political parties will recite a litany of what they did on behalf of the poor, underprivileged, and underserved, the record will show that they have also done more for the privileged, powerful, and influential segment of society—that segment with special interests, deep pockets, and the willingness to contribute to campaign coffers. In short, neither politicians nor political parties honestly care about or represent the people.

Nevertheless, the people expect to be represented. We expect our needs, hopes, and dreams to matter to our leaders; and, just as important, we expect them to care about our values and opinions. Leaders in government, whether at the village, city, county, state, or national level, are elected to represent the people—that is, to speak for us and reflect our opinions and wishes. Leaders in government are not elected to tell us what our values and opinions are or should be, or to disregard us because our needs, hopes, and dreams are not in line with theirs or in the majority.

A Lakota village council in the old days was called *wicahcala omniciye,* or "gathering of old men." The label aptly described them because the members of the council were no longer physically capable of taking to the field as warriors. Although their physical abilities may have diminished, they had acquired other characteristics that were just as important to the survival and growth of the community: They had gained experience and wisdom, which enabled them to understand that their place on the council was not a personal stepping-stone, but a solemn duty to the people—all the people. Furthermore, individual members of the council were known as *woglaka wicasa*, meaning "the man who speaks," which named their duty to speak for the people.

There were two critical factors relative to the relationship between the gathering of old men and the people. First, none of the members of the council were elected. They earned the right to be members by achieving elder status. Therefore their only allegiance was to the welfare of their village or community. Second, there was an effective deterrent to overt favoritism or politics—the right of individual free choice in Lakota society. Although the council had considerable experience and nearly limitless wisdom, no one in the community was obligated to listen to its opinions or advice. Most people did listen, of course, because the council took its responsibility seriously and its members were not out to gain fame, material rewards, or favorable ratings, or to show up well in polls.

Of course, some people today would argue that this system or arrangement is simplistic and primitive and would never work in today's complex world. That is debatable, but at least one concept is not: selfless commitment to the welfare of the people, which should not be misconstrued as archaic. In fact, it should have a place in any society, no matter how complex. Furthermore, the complexity of any society should not be a convenient excuse for its leaders not to practice and epitomize basic human values, such as dedication, commitment, honesty, and selflessness.

It is entirely possible that much of the complexity of our world today is an illusion projected by our use of and dependence on technology. In any case, many realities have remained as simple, basic, and harsh as they ever were, such as hunger, disease, ignorance, bigotry, greed, and apathy. Technology may enable the immediate care of the wounded or sick, but it apparently cannot infuse us with enough compassion to care about their quality of life once they are "well." That travesty cannot be corrected by complex technology, but only by the human will, and someone has to lead the way to the solution. That is why we need consistent leadership based on the best of basic human values.

A nation reflects the values of its people, and so it follows that the government of a nation should be an insight into the people it represents. A nation or a society without values produces leaders without character. Therefore, people in leadership positions, especially those who feel entitled to the position they hold, should be everyone's concern. Leaders influence and shape attitudes every day with every act, every failure to act, every pronouncement, every scandal, and every vote. It would be unwise to think, however, that leadership is the exclusive domain of the heads of state or elected officials. If we narrow our view and definition of leaders to only those people with titles, the consequences may not be to our liking.

Life happens on many levels and in many areas other than at the national level or on the world stage. People from all walks of life face issues and circumstances every day that governments, kings, prime ministers, governors, and presidents cannot solve and may not be equipped to handle. For this reason, leadership is just as necessary at the "everyday" level.

East of the foothills of a mountain range, an exceedingly deep gorge split the plain as it meandered out of the mountains and stretched for more than 125 miles. In an isolated region of the plains were two small towns, one on the north side of the gorge and the other on the south. More than a mile south of it was Gardenia, situated on a fertile plateau that allowed the townspeople to raise a variety of grain crops. A cold, rushing stream bustled out of the mountains and poured into the gorge from the north, where the town of Hum was situated on its banks, populated by tradesmen, such as carpenters, bricklayers, and blacksmiths.

The farmers of Gardenia had to travel roughly 60 miles to sell their grain crops after every harvest season, and often had difficulty repairing their farm tools and implements without the help of tradesmen. The people of Hum had a similar problem, as many had to travel to other towns in the region to find work, because their own town was so isolated.

One day the mayors of the two towns met at a narrow spot along the gorge, as they did often, each on his side. On this day they lamented the difficulties of the citizenry of their two towns and what they had to contend with to make a living. Over the years, friendships had formed and continued among the people from both sides of the gorge. They would meet at the gorge and visit, but of course they could not cross it because it was very, very deep. Climbing down one side and up the other was out of the question, because the walls were too steep. So the people would shout their conversations back and forth.

As the two mayors sat across from each other, they said (as they had on many occasions) that the gorge was preventing their two towns from engaging in commerce. Then Mayor Box of Hum said that it was really not the gorge that kept them apart—it was their inability to solve the problem. Both mayors gasped, because it was the most profound statement either of them had ever made. Then Mayor Short of Gardenia, inspired by his colleague's insight, said that they must do something to solve the problem. It was a banner day.

Word went out in both towns that something would be done to solve the problem of the gorge. Most of the people did not know exactly what that meant or what would happen. The gorge was not often the topic of conversation in either town. It was there and always had been, an obstinate reality of life for the people in both towns.

The elders of Hum sent word across to the elders of Gardenia to meet at the gorge. So they met and talked about what should be done, and the most popular consensus was that a bridge should be built across the gorge. After the bridge was finished, then a grinding mill could be built along the powerful stream that flowed from the mountains. That stream could be used to power the mill. The farmers of Gardenia could bring their grain over the bridge to be ground in the mill. In turn, the blacksmiths of Hum could cross the bridge and repair and refurbish farm implements and tools. It was another banner day.

After the excitement died away, the mayors were confronted with the question of just how to build a bridge, because that was the first part of the *solution. If a bridge could not be built, there was no use in building a mill. Days passed but no one could think of how to overcome this monumental hurdle. Conversations hummed in the bars and cafes of the towns, but no one had even the smallest of ideas or suggestions. Then one day a young merchant named Green approached Mayor Box of Hum with something of a plan.*

Merchant Green wanted to be appointed as head of the bridge project. Then he would travel around the region and talk to people to gather information on bridge building. He would bring that information back and he and the mayor would study the data and then decide on a plan. And finally, the shopkeeper would draw the plans for the bridge, and then hire men to build it. Of course, the towns of Hum and Gardenia would have to pay him for his services as head of the bridge project, for his information-gathering travels, and for building the bridge.

Mayor Box raised a yellow flag atop his city hall, a signal that meant he wanted to talk to the mayor of Gardenia. When the mayors arrived at the gorge, they were taken aback by an unexpected sight. On the ground near the south edge of the gorge were two very large and long pine logs. Each log had the girth of a barrel, but the most astonishing fact was that no one knew how they had gotten there. Merchant Green came to the gorge, and though he was as astonished as everyone else, he scoffed and walked away. The logs were of no consequence to him.

Though mystified by the logs, the mayors discussed the young merchant's plan, and gave it serious consideration because it was the only plan anyone had proposed. Confidently, Merchant Green waited. But two mornings later there was another surprise: two more long pine logs. The first pair was only a curiosity, but the second pair turned the logs into a mystery. Large crowds rushed to see as word got out, as if the logs would suddenly disappear before they could lay eyes on them.

People on both sides stared and gawked at the logs, and offered numerous theories on how they had come to be there. Anything from giants to spirits was blamed, or credited, until someone saw deep

*wheel tracks in the ground along the south side of
the gorge, with hoof prints of large draft horses.
Speculation grew wilder thereafter, because the
tracks came from the pine and alder forest south
of Gardenia.*

*The young merchant, now worried that the mystery of
the logs at the gorge would divert attention from his
proposal, pressed the mayors to approve his plan. On
the day the would-be bridge builder departed north in
his one-horse surrey, a man arrived from the pine and
alder forest with two more pine logs, all smaller than
the first four. Cautioning the people on the south side
to move aside, he turned his large wagon drawn by a
team of powerful horses and stopped near the edge of
the gorge. There he set about unloading his logs.*

*Curious onlookers watched the man work, but none
offered to lend a hand. Nevertheless, the man, who
was not young and not unfamiliar to some of the
people, finished his task alone. He had returned to
Gardenia only recently and built a log house for his
family. He was known for his quiet demeanor,
although there were rumors that the man, whose*

name was Talman, had been a soldier and had fought in a foreign war. But the few times he was asked, he only smiled and went on his way. Not once did he offer a word of explanation as he unloaded the logs and rolled them into place next to the others. Finally, one onlooker, who could no longer contain his curiosity, asked Talman why he had brought the logs to the gorge. He replied simply, "I will build a bridge."

Excitement reached a fever pitch in both towns. At sunset the next day, Talman returned to unload two more logs. Among the crowd of curious onlookers were Mayors Box and Short, both concerned that Talman's efforts would be a further drain on the treasuries of the towns. Furthermore, he had not been authorized to build a bridge. After all, Merchant Green was even now gathering information to draw up plans. When Mayor Short asked what he might bill for his work, Talman simply replied, "Nothing."

The mayors were stunned, uncertain what to do. Meanwhile, Talman continued to work. Every other day, Talman returned from the pine and alder forest with a load of logs, until there was a large pile of over

*two dozen of various lengths and thicknesses. Early
one morning, he arrived with two other men, who
appeared every bit as strong and competent as
Talman. First they took and recorded measurements.
Talman measured the width of the gorge by tossing
the end of a rope across to a boy. It was nearly thirty
meters across at a narrow spot. After that, he marked
all the logs at varying lengths and he and his helpers
began sawing logs and shaping wedged and flat ends
with axes.*

*Merchant Green, meanwhile, had also been busy. He
found several types of bridges and made sketches, but
he had also spent much of his time making inquiries
in bazaars and town squares, seeking men who had
experience building bridges. Not until the fourth town
he visited did he find anyone. The young merchant
dined with a man who had been recommended to
him, questioned him thoroughly until he was satisfied
that the man's knowledge was genuine, and then
hired him as his chief builder. Confident that he had
solved the problem for the towns of Hum and
Gardenia, Merchant Green was thinking that he
would open a shop in Gardenia with the profits from*

building the bridge. Furthermore, he knew he could convince Mayor Hum to hire him to build the mill. On a cold morning, the young merchant and his new chief builder departed for Hum.

At the gorge, the work progressed. Each day, Talman and his helpers arrived at sunrise and worked until sunset. All the bark from each log was peeled away, and each log was cut to a specific length, according to Talman's plans. The onlookers were surprised when Talman and his crew built a frame on the edge of the gorge, a hoist to raise and lower heavy logs using a block-and-tackle system. Next, they built a rope bridge across the chasm.

The activity at the gorge was the most exciting thing to happen to the people of Hum and Gardenia in many years. People rose early and stayed the day long to watch. Women brought food and drink for Talman and his crew. Anticipation hung in the air. One afternoon, one of the men was lowered into the gorge by ropes. At the depth of about 10 feet he chiseled ledges into the stone wall of the gorge. After crossing over on the rope bridge, he chiseled ledges at the same depth *on the opposite rock wall. It was evident to the onlookers that Talman and his men knew what they were doing. And some asked why this had not happened long ago.*

Merchant Green returned to Hum and soon heard the news. He hurried to the gorge and saw the crowds watching the activity. That evening, he found Mayor Box and demanded an explanation. The men working in the gorge were building a bridge, at no cost to either of the towns, reported the mayor. Merchant Green was incensed, reminding the mayor of their agreement, explaining that he had hired a man to build the bridge. But there was simply nothing to be done. Mayor Box had the town treasurer pay the young merchant for his travels and would hear no more argument. To make matters worse, the man hired by Merchant Green decided to help Talman.

The next day, an inverted V support frame, two logs attached end to end, was lowered into the gorge, wedged into the ledges that had been carved, and tied securely into place. The next day, an identical frame was lowered into place parallel to the first; then cross-

*beams were attached from one frame to the other.
Talman explained that the frames would support the
long beams that would span the gorge. Two days later,
the first main beams were laid across, resting on the
support beams and on the edges of the gorge on either
end. All that remained was for logs to be split into
planks and nailed in place.*

*By now the entire populations of both towns had come
to witness the finishing touches on the bridge made of
pine logs. After the planks for the decking were laid,
long railings were put into place. Then Talman and
his crew spent an entire day inspecting every joint,
every brace, and every fastener, climbing over and
crawling under the structure. To assure everyone of
the soundness of the bridge, Talman hitched his horses
to a wagon and drove it across from the south side to
the north and back again.*

*Some of the people were still skeptical, until Talman
invited the mayors to meet in the middle. There,
Mayor Box of Hum and Mayor Short of Gardenia
clasped hands, for the first time ever. Most of the
people on either side of the gorge crossed, too, however*

tentatively, resulting in an impromptu celebration. The citizens of Hum walked, ran, and drove to the town of Gardenia and were greeted with gifts, and the next day the citizens of Gardenia visited Hum and were welcomed with equal neighborliness and enthusiasm. The barrier of the gorge was no more.

A more formal celebration followed a few days later, and Talman and his crew were honored, including the man hired by Merchant Green. Though asked to make a speech to mark the occasion, Talman politely declined. After a closed-door meeting, the mayors decided to hire him to supervise the construction of the grinding mill. Of course, Talman accepted the job.

The grinding mill was built under Talman's steady guidance, and in time the dream of mutually beneficial commerce between the people of Hum and Gardenia was realized. After he finished building the grinding mill, Talman's skill as a builder of log houses was in almost constant demand. Consequently, he and his helpers built dozens and dozens of new homes in both towns. Now and then he was approached to stand for election as mayor of Gardenia, but he

*politely declined each time. He was embarrassed
when the log bridge was dubbed the Talman Bridge,
even though it had not been officially named.*

*Fifteen years after it was built, the pine log bridge
was replaced with a larger and stronger one made of
iron arches. The mayors had approached Talman and
asked him to supervise construction of the iron
bridge, but he declined. He knew nothing of working
with iron, he explained, suggesting that the blacksmiths might be more qualified. After a bridge archi-
tect was hired to draw up the plans, the blacksmiths
of Hum were indeed an integral part of the new
project, producing the various components for the new
bridge. Not surprisingly, Talman was immensely
relieved when the new iron bridge was named the
Hum-Gardenia Bridge.*

*Young Merchant Green did open a new shop in
Gardenia, and in a few years became one of the
wealthier citizens of Hum. He did stand for election
as mayor and won in a close vote. He was reelected
twice, each time by a closer vote. His entrepreneurial
skills were a benefit to the town, but his unfortunate*

habit of hiring only his closest friends for civic projects ended his political career.

When the log bridge was dismantled, Talman asked to have the old logs. By then he was a grandfather. He milled the logs into boards and built a gazebo in the Gardenia town square. There, on sunny summer days, people would sit and reminisce, and some would tell the story of how the first bridge across the gorge was built.

The story is, of course, fictional, but it is similar in many respects to situations and circumstances that occur in everyday life throughout the world. The necessity of solving problems to reach objectives is just as relevant to one or two villages as it would be to an entire nation.

There are several lessons on leadership in the story, as there are in real life. While the people assumed for many years that the gorge was the obstacle, one of the mayors finally ascertained that the real problem was the people's inability to overcome it. The bridge builder then appeared, not to order and direct, but to show the way. Therein is the hallmark of true leadership.

One is a good leader when what he says is validated by experience and what he does is validated by character. Every elected official, legislative body, board of directors, or organization, corporate, or company head leads by example whether he realizes it or not. Unfortunately, in some cases these people demonstrate how *not* to do or be something. Truth be told, perhaps there are too many of those examples. We should, therefore, put this question before anyone who thinks he is a leader: How should you influence the actions and attitudes of others?

Much speculation and theorizing could go into answering this question, but the pre-reservation Lakota distilled their expectations into a simple, elegant set of criteria. Crazy Horse took the oath to uphold their vision, as did many other great men before him. Today's leaders from all walks of life would do well to give serious consideration to the duties and responsibilities expected of a Shirt Wearer:

To wear the Shirt, you must be men above all others. You must help others before you think of yourselves. Help the widows and those who have little to wear and to eat, and have no one to speak for them. Do not look down on others or see those who look down on you, and do not let anger guide your mind or your heart. Be generous, be wise, and show fortitude so that the people can follow what you do and then what you say. Above all, have courage and be the first

*to charge the enemy, for it is better to lie a
warrior naked in death than to be wrapped up
well with a heart of water inside.*

Let us now consider these expectations one item at a
time, so that we might better understand how they apply
to our own experience:

To wear the Shirt, you must be men above all others.
It is not said here that once men (or women) achieve or
win a position of leadership, they must exalt themselves
or think of themselves as better or higher than everyone
else. Rather, to be "above all others" here means that
leaders must strive to represent the best that their
community, society, or nation stands for, such as selflessness, humility, generosity, sacrifice, and compassion. It
means that none should become leaders for the prestige
or rewards of leadership.

**You must help others before you think of yourselves.
Help the widows and those who have little to wear
and to eat, and have no one to speak for them.**
These lines state clearly that the needs of the leader are
secondary to the needs of the people—and the needs of
those who are less fortunate in any way should be the

first priority. Leaders should be as poor as the poorest who follow them, because all that they have materially should be given away to those who need it. Those whose voices are small or unheard because of their station or class must be heard first and always by their leaders.

Do not look down on others or see those who look down on you, and do not let anger guide your mind or your heart.

This means that a leader's status does not place him or her above anyone else, and that he or she must regard and treat everyone equally. Leaders must be big enough—or confident enough in the truth about themselves—to disregard any who condescend to or belittle them in any manner. Anger, retribution, and selfishness to any extent must never enter their minds, no matter the criticism or ridicule. In all circumstances and in all endeavors, especially when acting on behalf of and in the name of the people, anger must never be an influence.

Be generous, be wise, and show fortitude so that the people can follow what you do and then what you say.

Here, in one line, are three virtues considered by Lakota society to be most important: generosity, wisdom, and fortitude. Leaders are expected to be generous with their time, talents, and material resources. They are expected to speak and act wisely and seek guidance from those who are wiser, to the point of setting aside their own egos. Whatever their shortcomings might be, quitting cannot be one of them. Leaders are expected to remain steadfast in all things.

Actions are more substantive than words. If this is not a universal truth, then there are none. Leaders who are consistently generous, wise, and steadfast will achieve a level of credibility that can only be obtained by the effect of what they have done. Then, and only then, will what they have to say carry any weight. These actions are necessary not because they are expected of leaders, but because they are the foundation on which the society is based.

Above all, have courage and be the first to charge the enemy, for it is better to lie a warrior naked in death than to be wrapped up well with a heart of water inside.

Courage is just as important as generosity, wisdom, and fortitude. It is one of the four greatest virtues in Lakota society. To act courageously on behalf of the people is— or should be—more highly regarded than the accumulation of material wealth. Any who make the ultimate sacrifice, the "last full measure of devotion," will live on in the hearts and minds of many generations to come, while those who devote their lives to the accumulation of wealth will be forgotten.

The duties and responsibilities of Shirt Wearers were daunting, to say the least. Yet, as mentioned before, no compensation or authority came with the position; the responsibility itself was honor enough. The over-whelming majority of men who were given the distinc-tion accepted it in humility and took it seriously. Some were more successful than others in living up to the responsibilities, of course, which is proof that leadership in any society, in any age, is not easy.

The Lakota high standards for leadership were based on three realities. First, they understood that leaders are fallible human beings and would sometimes—or perhaps frequently—fail. Second, leaders were selected to serve the people first and foremost. And third, leaders were to reflect the values and the will of the people, not impose their own on others.

Crazy Horse devoted his life to these standards. His legacy can be an inspiration to us all.

AFTERWORD:
TO BE A LEADER

Of all of humankind's institutions, leadership is one of the oldest. Early humans banded together in loose enclaves to increase their odds for safety and survival. Sooner or later, someone stepped up to oversee to the collective good or impose his will to benefit himself. In one scenario, leadership was based on reason. In another, it was force or the threat thereof. Or perhaps the façade of reason was backed by the threat or use of force, or the threat of harm to the common good served as motivation to others to follow he who was best at mitigating it. Whatever his tactics, a person became the leader either by showing that his abilities consistently lent to the fulfillment of common objectives, or that his force could not be contested. And while reason is obviously preferable to brute force, any dictator or street gang has found violence to be the quicker and, sometimes, more apparently effective—especially when one's goals are selfish in nature.

Strong leadership has been a major factor in the survival, growth, or decline of societies and nations. List names such as Genghis Khan, Winston Churchill, Napoléon Bonaparte, Simón Bolívar, Indira Gandhi, Thomas Jefferson, François "Papa Doc" Duvalier, Queen Kamaeamaya, Benito Mussolini, Georges Clemenceau, or Franklin D. Roosevelt and we probably know whether their tenure was beneficial or harmful to their respective nations. Furthermore, in most instances these leaders' impact was felt beyond the borders of their countries. And we should not overlook the fact that even seemingly ineffectual leaders had (and have) some impact.

For the most part, however, leaders have not always been the choice of the people they led, or at least not the choice of all of the people. Those mentioned above were either elected, inherited power, or gained it by force. Dictators cared little (if at all) about popular support, and monarchs by and large did not have to depend on it to maintain their power. In the world's democracies, it is interesting though perhaps not surprising to note that in national elections there has never been a unanimous choice.

This observation may be somewhat trite, since population levels, political persuasions, racial and ethnic diversity, voter apathy, and social and economic class (among other factors) are too disparate to allow a unanimous election to be even remotely possible in this day and age. However, that also speaks to the fact that politicians will probably never consistently appeal to even a solid majority of the electorate; so they set their sights on appealing to at least 51 percent in a head-to-head contest.

Furthermore, it is somewhat difficult to believe that the politicians who stand for election in the democratic countries of the world are the best each country has to offer in terms of leadership material. As many people have thought or articulated, perhaps those who are truly qualified are also too smart to subject themselves to the contentious process. Or perhaps the reason for this is that the process itself, being more or less a popularity contest for politicians, does not focus on basic character values, such as honesty and humility or selflessness. But most of us forget that a shrewd politician does not a good—or even an adequate—leader make.

One of the most frequent comments from rank-and-file voters in recent American elections has been that they feel they are forced to choose the lesser of two evils. Such a choice obviously does not bode well for the governmental function of a given county, state, or nation. And it points out that politicians know how to work the system to win elections and acquire positions of power and influence. But the reality is that the process continues because the people allow it. We have not yet fully realized that life's realities transcend the egos of politicians who think they are entitled to the power and prestige of being county commissioners, senators, mayors, governors, and presidents. We have not yet fully realized that we need true leaders, not politicians who win popularity contests.

Democratic societies and nations have created governments that are as good and fair as any government man has developed, at least as far as the philosophy of fair representation is concerned. So without a doubt the failure to put truly qualified people in positions of leadership rests on the shoulders of the people themselves. It would behoove us as individuals to learn and understand how leaders are chosen, and how they are able to use the system now in place to rise to power.

Unfortunately, politicians are too much like germs that develop immunity to proven vaccines. Yet, just as medicine works to find ways to counteract germs, the general public must find ways to circumvent or alter the process to wrest control from the politicians and the lobbyists. After all, the people elect officials and representatives to reflect their values and their wishes. It is up to us to ensure that the elected are true leaders.

We humans have managed to fashion our societies into complex technocracies and our lives into convoluted journeys. By and large we consider complexity to be a good thing. The more complex and complicated we are, the more civilized—or so we assume. But in the process we have also managed to complicate an extremely critical aspect of our societies, one that now affects us day in and day out, and will affect future generations as well. That aspect is the process by which we select our leaders.

In some cases, the leaders have literally chosen themselves, which usually turns out tragically for the people. Fortunately, however, many of the world's nations have the freedom to choose their leaders. While that is immeasurably precious, there is one downside: We have politicized the process to the extent that elected officials are referred to as *political leaders*. We have forgotten that politics and leadership are two separate and very different things!

Just as there are leaders in all walks of life—such as in religion, education, science, the arts, and so on—most every profession or organization has its own politics. Yet the president of a professional organization or a labor union is not referred to as a *political* leader. But those government leaders who impact every person and every organization in the country are, which should be a significant concern for every free-thinking adult in the country. It means that we have come to accept the fact that the leaders we depend on to be ethical, moral, compassionate, and honest (among other things) are politicians first. As we know, politics is not exactly a hotbed of ethics, morality, compassion, or honesty.

The average citizen by and large wants good leaders. However, one significant obstacle stands in the way. In this country the people do not have the primary influence in selecting candidates to stand for election. The system ensures that politicians and political parties have the power to choose the candidates in every election, and then they place the candidates in front of the voting public. Consequently, voters are forced to accept the slate of candidates in spite of any doubts and reservations they may have. Third-party or independent candidates have never been successful: for any draft candidate to have credibility, he or she would have to be a member of a major political party—which is akin to a committee of foxes guarding the henhouse.

To put good leaders in office, the voters must take control of the election process, starting with a rigid set of standards by which to assess all candidates. Obviously there are legal qualifications that all candidates must meet, but the voter standards for candidates should be higher, and any candidate's membership in a political party should be irrelevant.

Currently, when all is said and done, voters elect the politician that has done the best job of convincing them that he or she is the right person for the job. What has really transpired is that voters have accepted someone's promises to be a good leader, and then they cross their fingers and hope that the promises they bought into will be kept. And at this point in the process, hope is all that the voters have, because in the cold harsh glare of reality, in electing most of the politicians in public office they have taken a serious gamble.

Taking a gamble on unproven leaders is a symptom of a political system—and that means voters—that cares little if at all for real problems in the real world. While politicians work to keep their jobs instead of doing their jobs, the everyday issues and problems are as basic and elemental as they ever were: hunger, ethnocentrism, greed, disease, bigotry, genocide, warmongering, anthropocentrism, apathy, homelessness, and the list goes on.

Any system of government that advertises itself to be "of the people, by the people, and for the people" has a legal and moral obligation to honor that simple but powerful principle. Too often, however, it is government "of the people" to the exclusion of "by" and "for."

For example, although approximately 70 percent of the American people disapproved of the war in Iraq, the U.S. government nevertheless chose to forge ahead with its goals, refusing to let the will of the public be a part of the overall consideration of the issue. True leadership reflects the values and wishes of the people; anything else is merely politics or pandering to the selfish needs of a privileged few. Unfortunately this happens more often than not and is becoming the norm, which means it is no longer an obvious exception or anomaly.

Successful leadership has allowed human societies to achieve specific goals or objectives—more wealth, more power, more land, more resources, more control over resources or other people, more military buildup, spreading our beliefs (thereby eliminating other belief systems), and so on. By that definition, we have tended to view anyone who can lead a group or a nation to achieve those objectives as a good leader. Never mind the fact that pursing those objectives often means using fear, ethnocentrism, bigotry, greed, genocide, anthropocentrism, and warmongering as tools to achieve the desired results. . . .

For example, someone espouses a radically different ideology than ours, so we convince everyone that unless we do something about him or her, he or she will change the world, and that will be bad for us.

After all, we feel threatened that we'll have to learn another language or be forced to worship in a different way. So we make everyone afraid and unite them under a banner of fear. Or someone has grievously insulted us and it becomes necessary to put him or her back in his or her place—which is obviously subservient to us. We cannot let anyone forget who we are. Or, perhaps some people have a valuable resource that we need and deserve; and of course, they do not deserve to have it because they are not as good and powerful as we are. Therefore, it is acceptable to take what we need and deserve by means of attrition, without factoring in collateral damage to the innocent or powerless, or the natural environment.

We modern humans think of ourselves as superior versions of our ancestors. While it may be true that on the average we are physically taller and larger, the jury will be out for some time as to whether or not we have improved as a species. Meanwhile, we still must contend with the same basic issues our ancestors did: food, shelter, clothing, and security. Of course, the ways to procure or acquire them have changed. In the past, people gathered, planted, hunted, and fished in order to have food, clothing, and shelter; and that required skills that an overwhelming majority of the human race does not have today.

As a result, we modern humans have forgotten that we are basically predatory by nature. Our ancestors had to hunt and gather food to survive. Those instincts have not been entirely bred out of us. We are still hard-wired to pursue and take, and that means killing and destroying what we need for food, shelter, and clothing, and to ensure our safety and security. Those instincts drive us more than we realize, and since we are social creatures—or herd animals—our ultimate strength lies in numbers. The more of us that can work together to achieve an objective, the better our chances are for success. Though most of us are aware of that fact, we frequently do not act on our own accord until we are convinced by a few to follow behind them to pursue or support an objective. No matter how sophisticated or complicated we think we are, we still have the same basic needs as our ancestors; therefore, "leaders" can use the same methods to influence us.

We must always remember that the word *leader* carries with it the implication of opposite characteristics: bad or good, weak or strong, wrong or right, selfish or selfless, arrogant or humble, and so forth. The characterization obviously depends on the individual leader and, more important, what the leader does. Most leaders are astute enough to be in tune with our needs, our opinions, and our expectations, and most leaders will play to them in the rhetoric they use to win our support. If that rhetoric leads to substantive action that has positive consequences for the people, we are pleased. But there is that fine line between what the leader does to benefit certain groups and what he or she does for the greatest good of all or most of the people.

Leaders may be complex as individuals, but leadership does not need to be complicated. Neither does it have to be limited to predominantly serve the negative aspects of human pursuits, nor to serve the needs of only a few. In a democratic society we have a right to expect our leaders to reflect the best of what we are as a nation. And in the corporations, organizations, and communities of which we are a part, we have the responsibility to ensure that leadership upholds the same standards.

Good leaders and good leadership are necessary in every walk of life. No organization can hope to function and accomplish its purpose or mission without them. In every field there are two broad categories of employees or volunteers: those individuals who meet the basic or minimal requirements to keep their jobs and pass performance reviews, and those whose performance and attitude is beyond the curve. Therefore, the question must be asked: Who are the leaders in this scenario? The answer is not as simple as it may seem.

Although administrators, managers, and such have broader responsibilities, not all of them can be considered leaders. In reality, the people in these positions of authority influence the actions and attitudes of others. Therefore, our concern should be to ensure that their influence is positive and dynamic. If they are simply resting on their laurels and cashing in on their position, then these people are not being good leaders. Every organization needs those individuals whose performance and attitude exceeds job descriptions and expectations. Those are the true leaders, even if their titles do not accurately reflect this status. Those kinds of people put in more hours, work harder, see the big picture clearly, and make things happen, to say the least. They lead by example.

Not everyone is born to be a leader, but anyone who so chooses can prepare himself or herself to lead when the moment comes. That moment may come more often than we realize, or whether we want it or not. It is probably a safe bet that Rosa Parks did not wake up one morning and make a conscious decision to do something to change the world. But when the moment came, she did not turn away. She relied on her instincts and her values—in other words, her character—to confront the issue at hand, which was whether or not to give up her seat and give in once more to the rules of segregation and racism. It is also a safe bet that Rosa Parks did not consider herself to be a leader, certainly not in the same category as Dr. Martin Luther King Jr. But because she stubbornly exhibited quiet fortitude in an extremely difficult and dangerous moment, she set an example for every downtrodden person in the world.

Rosa Parks did something beyond take a stand. She demonstrated leadership at its simplest and most effective level. She showed that true leadership is predicated on what we do. No matter how often we say "Do as I say" to anyone, it is what we do that has the most impact and meaning.

But Rosa Parks should also be an example for every governor, mayor, president, king, legislator, member of Parliament, police chief, religious leader, and everyone who has the audacity to think of themselves as leaders. Anyone can assume or be elected or be appointed to a position that is vested with authority; and anyone can hide behind that authority, especially when there is a stated or implied threat of punishment. That is why it is easier to influence people by invoking fear. But it takes an individual with character to truly lead. It takes a person with character to demonstrate that quiet fortitude can be more powerful than fear.

Value-based character can be more powerful than authority. Authority can be lost or taken away or diminished, but character will remain steadfast. Former U.S.

president Jimmy Carter has arguably done more good works as a private citizen than he did with the considerable might and authority he had as a sitting president. The celebrity of being president certainly helped, but it was and is his character that is now his source of power and influence.

Rosa Parks and Jimmy Carter are certainly examples of selfless leadership. Every society, every nation needs leaders like these in every walk of life to put the needs of others ahead of their own. These are the kind of leaders who understand the responsibility of the positions they hold and then honor that responsibility. They are the kind of leaders, especially elected officials, who do not feel entitled to the jobs they have. Such a person understands that doing the job is the best way to keep it.

In any society there will be those who are less fortunate. In Lakota society it was usually the widows and the elderly, whose households had no hunter. Since hunting was the primary method of procuring food, this was a serious predicament. The community—essentially the extended family—was aware, of course, of those situations, and the hunters in the village would provide meat for those who needed it.

One of the defining values consistently exhibited by Crazy Horse was his compassion for the weak and the powerless. It was what eventually drew people to him

as a leader, but he began demonstrating those tendencies as an adolescent. Probably at the urging of his
mother at first, he would hunt and take meat to the
families who had no one else to hunt for them. After
that, he willingly and frequently provided for the
elderly and anyone who needed it, to the extent that he
influenced other hunters to increase their own efforts
to do the same.

One expects a leader to act dynamically and hero-
ically. As a mature warrior and leader of fighting men,
Crazy Horse did exactly that. But his overall status as a
leader went far beyond the battlefield into the arena of
everyday life. To study his life is to have an insight into the
broad scope of leadership, which ranges from the quiet
acts to those that are the stuff of legend.

Our perception of leadership should not be limited
to or defined solely by a few acts of heroism. Such acts
are not to be diminished or dismissed, of course, but we
should understand that they are only part of the big
picture. Leadership happens every day in every situation, as we face issues and circumstances within the
context of real life. While single spectacular events do
capture attention and headlines, the seemingly mundane
struggles can have just as much of an impact on the
world. This is because they test the values, beliefs, and
character of the ordinary people who are the backbone
of every society.

To understand this truth, we must understand that history is not shaped solely by the individuals to whom we give the credit—the Sitting Bulls or George Washingtons. That is to say that while the role and impact of great leaders is undeniable, they could never have achieved their victories alone. Rather, it has often been the nameless and forgotten followers who have provided the impetus to a leader's philosophy, or put themselves in harm's way and thus enabled the leaders to be given the credit. It has been the ordinary people, who are much more in touch with the realities of everyday life, who have affirmed their societies' norms and values and signaled the need for change.

If nothing else, Crazy Horse was one of the people. His sense of humility would not allow him to think otherwise, and Lakota society was always there to remind him that being a leader was a position of responsibility and not privilege. Indeed, as a leader he did not have unlimited authority, special privileges, or prosperity. He did not limit his leadership to dynamic acts on the field of battle. He was there to face life day in and day out just like anyone else. As a warrior, he did set himself apart and demonstrated courage and steadiness under duress, which was what convinced the people that he possessed the qualities of a good leader. But his skills and bravery on the battlefield were augmented by his character, which reflected the community and society of which he was a part.

Crazy Horse did not lead by issuing orders or making pronouncements. He did not lead because he was much better than anyone else or by setting himself above others. His lodges were not bigger or taller, nor did he have more than anyone else. His horses were not better, faster, or more expensive than anyone else's. As a matter of fact, his herd was smaller than most because he gave horses away to those who needed them.

Crazy Horse consistently exhibited the most effective methods of leadership. He was certain of his skills and abilities and understood the risks of exceeding them, especially when the safety and welfare of the people hung in the balance. But he also understood that the safety and welfare of the people made it necessary to strive beyond his skills and abilities from time to time.

He picked his friends carefully and knew their skills and abilities and strengths and weaknesses as well as he knew his own. He knew who was capable in one area or for certain tasks or missions; and he knew that the way to invite defeat or failure was to ask anyone to perform beyond their capabilities. Likewise, Crazy Horse knew his enemies as well as he could and he never allowed ethnocentrism to interfere with his assessments. But he also knew there were enemies that did not carry lances or guns but were equally dangerous—those weapons included selfishness, arrogance, jealousy, hunger, apathy, loneliness, duplicity, indifference, and so forth. Most significantly, Crazy Horse knew that one of those enemies was inaction; so he consistently took the lead by setting the right example. He did it first before he asked anyone else to do the same.

Because he gave himself selflessly to his responsibility, Crazy Horse had a fervently loyal following both as a civilian and military leader. He did his best to see to the needs of all of the people, whether they liked him or not. From his family and community he learned the values that were the basis of Lakota society, and he did his best to live them in his personal life as well as in his role as leader. He was humble, dedicated, selfless, and persistent. And he did it all with humility. His own welfare, reputation, and standing—his image, if you will—was always secondary to the wishes and the welfare of the people. We should expect no less of ourselves in positions of leadership, or from the leaders who serve us today.